A Knight's Own Book of Chivalry

A Knight's Own Book of Chivalry

GEOFFROI DE CHARNY

Introduction by Richard W. Kaeuper

Translation by Elspeth Kennedy

PENN

UNIVERSITY OF PENNSYLVANIA PRESS

Philadelphia

THE MIDDLE AGES SERIES

Ruth Mazo Karras, Series Editor
Edward Peters, Founding Editor

A complete list of books in the series is available from the publisher.

10   9   8   7   6   5

Published by
University of Pennsylvania Press
Philadelphia, Pennsylvania 19104-4112

Library of Congress Cataloging-in-Publication Data
Charny, Geoffroi de, d. 1356.
A knight's own book of chivalry / historical introduction by Richard W. Kaeuper ;
translation by Elspeth Kennedy.
    [Livre de chevalerie. English]
    p.   cm.—(The Middle Ages series)
    Includes bibliographical references
    ISBN 0-8122-1909-0 (pbk. : alk. paper)
    1. Charny, Geoffroi de, d. 1356.   2. Livre de chevalerie.   3. Chivalry.   4. Knights and
knighthood.   5. Civilization, Medieval.   6. Courtly love.   I. Title.   II. Kaeuper,
Richard W.   III. Kennedy, Elspeth.   IV. Series
CR4513 .C43   2005
394′.7′0940902—dc22   2005042260

Contents

Historical Introduction to the Text

Reading Charny and Understanding Chivalry

GEOFFROI DE CHARNY (c.1306–1356) was the chivalric embodiment of his colorful and violent age. His adult life coincided with the opening phase of the series of Anglo-French conflicts we call the Hundred Years War (traditionally 1337–1483). He was also intensely pious and, in fact, was the first documented owner of the Shroud of Turin. A close look at this man's lively career as a knight and his unusual treatises about his profession offer fascinating insights. Charny opens up to us the set of ideas and practices that by his time dominated the lay elite and guided all who wanted to enter it. Geoffroi de Charny lived the vocation about which he wrote. Through his vigorous embodiment of these values he climbed swiftly into the inner circle of medieval French warriors. At the peak of his fame he died a hero's death under the swords of English and Gascon enemies at the decisive battle of Poitiers (1356), with the oriflamme (the sacred banner of the kings of France) clutched in his hand to the last. If we explore his career and read his major treatise (printed in English translation here), we can learn not only about knighthood, but about how a French warrior-aristocrat in the mid-fourteenth century could express his thoughts. Indeed we can learn what those thoughts were on a score of subjects, including a knight's relationship with God, the just rule of princes, the proper approach to death, the role of ladies in his male world, and even the moral laxity of newly fashionable clothing.

Yet it is chivalry that forms the central strand in Charny's life and books. He wants to instruct aspiring young knights in their high vocation and recall grizzled veterans to the ideal. Thus before constructing an overview of his career we need a sense of what medieval chivalry was and, equally important, what it was not.[1] We need to avoid both scholarly and popular misconceptions. Scholars sometimes mistakenly assert that there was nothing among the laity at all comparable to the structuring ideas and powerful ethos among the clergy. "There was no such thing as a lay *esprit de corps*," wrote the late Sir Richard Southern, an eminent and insightful historian who seldom made such mistakes.[2] In fact, chivalry provided the lay *esprit de corps* and served well as the ideological framework for lay society for nearly five centuries. While it is true that chivalry borrowed clerical ideas and imagery, it shaped them in its own image and undoubtedly retained a distinct lay identity.[3] Charny takes us at once into this mental and intensely physical world of chivalry. The issues addressed are significant: it was by chivalric ideas and through chivalric practices that elite lay folk organized their thoughts and directed action in basic categories of life. It was through the window of chivalry that they viewed violence and honor, piety, elite political and personal relationships, love and gender relationships, and rightful material possessions, to suggest even a partial list.

Medieval chivalry was thus a highly serious code. It was in no sense frivolous or ephemeral, concerned only with a few outward forms of social life as the popular notion would have it. This popular notion is largely formed from post-medieval revisions and revivals. To see genuine medieval chivalry clearly we must demolish the structures, many of them venerably Victorian, which stand in the way. Observing the increasingly rare phenomenon of a male opening a door for a woman or standing in respect when another person enters a room, modern observers may still be heard to mumble—either in praise or with irony—that chivalry is not dead. This longevity of chivalry is highly significant, but it creates distinct problems of interpretation. We may easily think that such pale modern survivals from the medieval code show us how chivalry actually worked in the medieval period. They do not. Student papers (and, let it be said, the textbooks students are set to read) often speak of "ideal" or "true" chivalry, assuming that this means the set of ideas praised by the Victorians and still honored by some die-hard followers in modern times. Some would prefer chivalry to be a set of ideals all could still like without qualification. They may be surprised to find how tough a warrior code the chivalry of medieval times was and how much it valued sheer prowess.

An idea of chivalry based on Victorian values will likewise distort our sense of the broad place of chivalry in medieval society. Chivalric ideals, it is again easy to think, surely went far toward solving the historical problems represented by vigorous masculinity in the Middle Ages. The rapidly developing society of Europe in the Central or High Middle Ages (roughly 1050–1300) sought to achieve new or renewed order in basic areas of life, political, social and intellectual. Rulers and intellectuals worried over the disruptive violence to which males were prone. The idealistic, Victorian view is that they achieved their goal through chivalry, by advancing standards of fair play, courtesy, and respect for women as the desirable but "weaker" sex. These ideas about the past may have enraptured our Victorian ancestors who wanted them to work in their own age; they have understandably provoked critical disbelief and even outrage in more recent thought.

If we are trying to understand chivalry as it functioned in the Middle Ages, we must wipe the slate clean and start with sound medieval evidence, not wishful thinking from any age. The *Book of Chivalry* is an excellent source for beginning that exploration. It was written by a practicing knight, one of the most renowned of his age. As we will see, it was likely intended for a body of practicing knights, the Order or Company of the Star, the new chivalric order of the king of France. The voice we hear speaking in this book is that of a knight, not a clerical reformer. Charny, we will discover, is in his own way a reformer, too; yet he writes always as a practicing warrior, giving practical advice to other practicing warriors in the real world. In the process he reveals how his fellow warriors thought and acted in their very real world, and also how he wanted them to think and act.

Other voices often heard on medieval chivalry are finally less directly revealing. A medieval cleric and scholar such as John of Salisbury (ca. 1115–1180) can, of course, tell us much about ideals for knighthood; but we must read his book with great care, understanding that his devotion to revered classical sources will bend medieval knights into shapes as much like Roman soldiers as possible.[4] Ramon Lull (ca. 1232–1316) had formerly been a knight, but even his great work on chivalry comes out of a scholarly study and from a time when he had left the practice of knighthood to become a quasi-friar.[5] Like John of Salisbury's works, Lull's book must be sifted through powerful filters to discover actual historical knighthood. Geoffroi de Charny is as close to the genuine voice of knighthood as we are likely to get.[6]

Charny's Career

Geoffroi de Charny's birth date likely falls in the early years of the four-teenth century, certainly before or during 1306, the date of his mother's death.[7] His first prominent appearances in 1337 suggest an age of maturity that would place his birth shortly before his mother's death. He was born into elite society, but not into its top ranks. He was a younger son in a family that was itself only tangentially linked to the great houses of his native Burgundy. In early adulthood he can have held little land. Through the reign of Philippe VI (1328–50) he most regularly resided at the castle of Pierre-Perthuis, an estate that came to him with his first marriage, to Jeanne de Toucy. Their marriage produced no surviving children and ended with Jeanne's death by 1342. By the end of his life, likely as a result of his second marriage—to Jeanne de Vergy, Lady of Montfort and Savoisy—he was lord not only of Pierre-Perthuis and Lirey but of Montfort and Savoisy. Their two children were Geoffroi, who became his heir, and Charlotte. Shortly before his death he also came into possession of two houses, one in Paris, through the gift of his sovereign, Jean le Bon.

Charny's career was shaped by first phase of the Hundred Years War (from Edward III's claiming the French throne in 1337 to the Treaty of Brétigny in 1360).[8] He was enthusiastically caught up in the fighting from his first major campaign in 1337 to his heroic death at his sovereign's side in 1356. The great conflict between the Valois kings of France and the Plantagenet kings of England provided the given in Charny's life. War was a setting in which he worked well, for, as the French medieval historian Raymond Cazelles has wisely observed, to live without an enemy to fight would be contrary to the spirit of chivalry Charny embodied.[9]

Even a brief account of Charny's military career over two decades shows that he had no difficulties in finding enemies to fight. Leading a small troop of five squires (*ecuyers*), he appeared in the southwest of the realm between July and October 1337, campaigning in Gascony under the Constable of France, Raoul, count of Eu (who seems to have been Charny's patron and whose wife was related to Charny's wife). He was then a new bachelor (*bachelier*), a young nobleman serving under a military captain, a banneret, because he lacked the means to supply his own sizable force for war.

As Edward III constructed a coalition of allies in the Low Countries, Charny's field of action shifted northward, to Flanders and Hainault. Again Charny regularly served under the Constable of France. In 1340 when Edward and his allies marched against Tournai, Charny was ordered by the French king, Philippe VI, to join in its defense. All the defenders won praise for their valor in saving the town, but Charny may well have felt disappointed that his king refused to fight the decisive pitched battle which the English seemed willing to hazard.

His was not the only dashed hope. The entire campaign was a disappointment to the English, who after a brief truce turned their attention to

Brittany where a dynastic quarrel offered new opportunities. Edward III backed one claimant, Jean de Montfort; Philippe VI backed the other, Charles de Blois. It comes as no surprise, then, to find Charny on the frontiers of Brittany in 1341, leading three *ecuyers* in the service of the Duke of Normandy, the future King Jean II of France. Charny's knightly qualities were already bringing him honor. When Charles de Blois came in September of 1342 to relieve Morlaix, besieged by the English under the Earl of Northampton, he gave Charny command of the first line of attacking cavalry. Honor, unfortunately for Charny, did not always mean success. His frontal charge, the classic French tactic, was thrown back and the second French wave rode straight into a defensive line of pits disguised by greenery. Some fifty French knights died and three times that number were captured, Charny among them. Richard Talbot, his English captor, sent Charny for honorable safekeeping to his principal residence, Goodrich castle in Herefordshire.[10] Perhaps Charny's military eye could appreciate the details of his captor's castle: the rock-cut ditch, the reddish stone walls and towers set with massive spurs, still visible today. Perhaps his eye could only look beyond the castle across green countryside stretching toward the distant Channel.

Charny did not pine long in captivity. He was evidently soon acquired as a prisoner by an even more powerful English lord who had taken part in the battle at Morlaix, William de Bohun, Earl of Northampton. Bohun quickly ransomed him—or at least released him from captivity to seek the money to pay his ransom. Charny's reputation had suffered not one whit. He had fought bravely and well. We know that by 1343 he had been knighted; he is termed a knight in both English and French governmental documents in this year.[11] We would like to know more—who knighted him, where, and when; but the evidence provides only the rough date for what must have been one of the most significant days in his life.

Charny was soon back in harness and was entrusted with new responsibility. In the closing months of 1342, after Edward III crossed the Channel in October to take personal command in the Breton theater, Charny acted as one of the marshals of the army coming to raise the siege of Vannes. Edward's army by this time had pillaged its way up to the town walls. Once again, however, the great open confrontation of armies failed to happen. In mid-January 1343 papal legates prevented an immediate and epic Anglo-French pitched battle and produced a truce not broken for a year and a half. The Hundred Years War had briefly shut down, as it often did.

Evidently dissatisfied with this period of military inactivity, Charny soon sought out new enemies in another field altogether. In 1345 he joined the crusade of Humbert II, dauphin of Viennois, directed against Smyrna in Anatolia.[12] The recent Christian capture of this fine port had produced a wave of crusading interest in the west. Humbert's force sailed from Marseilles to Genoa, crossed the Italian peninsula to Venice, and only after lengthy negotiations set sail again, arriving in Smyrna in June 1346—delayed by quarrels with Italian allies. In the end the entire effort, in Sir Steven Runciman's words, "had been singularly futile."[13] What Charny thought of battling the Turks we can guess; what he thought of the trials, perils, and inconveniences of a crusade shows up unmistakably in his another of his books, the *Charny Book* (*Livre Charny*), in which crusading appears as a form of quasi-martyrdom.

Charny and his men apparently returned to France in the summer of 1346, well before their leader Humbert returned in 1347. Had Charny hurried home after learning of the active reopening of the Anglo-French war? Humbert on his return to France gave up worldly struggle and entered a Dominican convent. Charny lost no time in re-entering the active struggle of Anglo-French warfare.

Charny missed the great set-piece battle of Crécy because he was engaged in other missions for his king. Under the Duke of Normandy he was part of the force again sent to the southwest to blunt the campaign of the English and their Gascon allies. Yet, as in 1340, a greater crisis for the French soon changed the location of Charny's military work. Edward III had again landed on the coast of France, this time in Normandy. He launched the campaign that would bring the great English victory at Crécy. At the time of this battle the chronicler Froissart places Charny among the heroic defenders of the town of Béthune, besieged by a Flemish army allied with the English. Charny's reputation probably benefited from his association with a successful defense at just the time when the host representing French chivalry in general had suffered a humiliating defeat at Crécy.

Following their triumph on that battlefield, the English went on to besiege the important port of Calais. The French king was vainly trying to find a way to pry open the English stranglehold on this strongly fortified town. His efforts were frustrated by the topography of the region (seacoast dunes exposed to fire from the English fleet, swampy land cut by frequent canals), as well as by the fortifications the English had built at vulnerable points. Philippe VI decided to send Edward a formal challenge to come out and fight. Charny's growing reputation led Philippe to choose him as one of two emissaries to convey the challenge to the English king. Charny and his colleague, the Lord of Montmorency, took mental notes on all the defenses they passed in reaching Edward III, but once they talked with the English king they could only take back a disappointing answer. Edward told them that Calais was his in right and would soon, after an expensive siege, be his in fact; if the king of France wanted to come to him he would have to find a way. This answer, of course, marked no stain on Edward's chivalric reputation. On the French side, Philippe's chivalry likewise led to no foolishness. He had no desire for a frontal assault over the difficult terrain and against the daunting fortifications seen first hand by Charny and Montmorency. The French army withdrew. Calais, its citizens starving, heroically held out six more weeks before the town surrendered in early August. It would be the English beachhead in France for the next two centuries.

The more immediate effect was to precipitate a political crisis in France. Philippe VI and his chief vassals had repeatedly failed to carry out the most elementary function of knights and feudal lords, the defense of their land. When, at the end of November 1347, Philippe of necessity summoned an assembly of the Estates of France to refill his war coffers, he had to listen to trenchant criticisms: the King had raised hosts of men at great cost and suffered humiliating defeat; he had been reduced to making truces with enemies still within his realm; he had been badly counseled. Such criticisms helped generate the current of reform that swept new men into the royal council, men who might bring about political and military success, men who might even be able to provide the new moral tone so necessary. God was obviously punishing the kingdom for sin.

Geoffroi de Charny figured among the several virtuous knights added to the council in this time of crisis and uncertainty; the king even arranged a residence in Paris for Charny as a convenient base for his new councilor and as a reward for his good and loyal services in the king's wars and other affairs. Charny had, in fact, for some time been as busy with diplomacy as with war. He had served, for example, as one of the group of French negotiators who secured a peace between Humbert II, Dauphin of Viennois, and the Count of Savoy. He had also helped to negotiate an Anglo-French truce in September 1347.

Yet he may well have likewise helped to formulate ambitious plans for a bold French counterstroke. France had been ravished by English invasions; now her leadership planned an elaborate invasion of England with massive financing, a strong force, portable forts and the like. Such military work would have undoubtedly been more congenial to Charny than rounds of diplomatic conversation. These plans for invasion soon dissolved, however, as France suffered an invader much more deadly than anything either Valois or Plantagenet could muster. The Black Death devastated France in 1348, killing on a scale beyond the capacity of warriors' weapons. The plague utterly disrupted the ambitious financial scheme designed to amass the needed war fund of more than three million livres.[14]

The war went on nonetheless, and Charny rode by order of Philippe VI to watch the military frontier from a base at St. Omer. Froissart says that for the business of war Charny functioned "like a king."[15]

Certainly he was second to none in his obsession to recover the great prize of Calais.[16] He conceived a plan to regain the town by bribing a Lombard named Aimery de Pavia, who was apparently a captain of its citadel (though Froissart inflates his position to that of governor of the town). Froissart says Charny reasoned that Aimery was not a man of high status, that he was not a native Englishman, and that (being a Lombard) he was greedy. Since it was a time of truce, contacts were easily established across the lines and negotiations begun.

Though Aimery had previously served Edward III loyally as a naval commander, he may have been tempted by Charny's offer of 20,000 écus. But he was also prudent. Froissart relates in one version of his chronicle that Aimery was called suddenly to London by King Edward, who had heard disturbing rumors. Aimery saved himself by telling all (from a suitable kneeling position) and by cooperating with Edward in setting a trap. In another version of his chronicle Froissart asserts that Aimery only pretended to negotiate with Charny and, at the right time, loyally informed Edward of the attempt to regain Calais by a bribe. In any event he soon returned to his negotiations with Charny. The exchange of castle and town for money was to take place in the waning hours of the last day of 1349.

Charny came prepared with the money and a sufficient force to hold Calais. Froissart pictures Charny and his close companions joking to ease their impatience while a few men carried in at least a large part of the money and saw to the opening of the gates. "That Lombard takes a long time," Charny is made to say, "He'll kill us with the cold." Charny insisted that he would ride, preceded by his banner, through the high gate before him, as soon as it was opened; he would not enter the low wicket-gate through which the small party passed in making the final arrangements. But while he and his men shivered in their cold armor, Aimery (who had securely stashed away his bribe) alerted a hidden but overpowering English force. Edward III had secretly reinforced the garrison at Calais and had then brought his son and a few trusted companions to join in springing the trap. The exact nature of this trap much exercised the chroniclers' creative powers. Geoffroy le Baker pictures the English, hidden behind a false wall cleverly joined to the solid stonework, suddenly bursting out on their enemies while a trusted man hurled a huge stone to smash the beams of the turning bridge, already cut nearly in two, thus trapping the French within the walls. While such details seem invented, the outcome is clear. Once this small French party within the castle was captured, the English swung open the outer gates and rushed the surprised force outside. Charny apparently shouted to his companions that they were betrayed and must stand and fight bravely. Most of the French force in fact fled, pursued rashly by Edward III leading what seems to have been a smaller force of knights and archers than those they pursued. A sharp fight ensued on a causeway leading through marshy ground; the herald of Sir John Chandos claimed that this was one of the king's hardest fights, and that the day was won for the English only by the entry into the combat of Edward the Black Prince and his men.[17] When the king's son arrived with English reinforcements, the French broke again and the fight was finished. Charny, who had apparently stood his ground, fell captive. He must have been cut through his helmet for he was suffering a head wound. The knight to whom he actually surrendered, John de Potenhale, would receive 100 marks from Edward III "for the good services by him performed for the said Lord the King, and especially for taking Geoffrey de Charny." Potenhale later personally conducted Charny to London at the king's expense.[18] Charny entered his second period of captivity; it can only have been as honorable in its conditions as it was frustrating in its enforced inactivity.

On the very night after the battle the captured French knights were treated to a classic chivalric display. They learned for the first time that they had fought Edward III in person; the English king had in fact fought in plain armor. Now he personally waited on his prisoners at the supper table. After the meal he mingled with his captive guests in friendly conversation. But his demeanor changed somewhat when he came to Charny. Froissart gives him a reproving speech:

Messire Geoffroy, Messire Geoffroy, I rightly owe you very little love since you wanted to take from me by night what I have won and what has cost me much money: so I am very pleased to have put you to the test. You wanted to get it more cheaply than I, for 20,000 écus; but God aided me so that you failed in your intent. He will yet aid me, if it pleases Him, in my greater endeavor.[19]

Edward's comments apparently left Charny little to say, so he stood in silence, listening with what one of the Froissart manuscripts describes as feelings of shame.[20]

Since shame was the feeling or condition most to be feared by an honorable knight, the issue is important. Had Charny violated a truce and reduced his honor by negotiating the seizure of Calais for mere money? Kervyn de Lettenhove, one of the prominent nineteenth-century editors of Froissart, provided a legalistic defense. Charny had not violated a truce because he had not personally negotiated it nor sworn to uphold it. After his release, he was careful to swear to uphold the current truce.[21] This argument may have some force, but of course the issue transcends legal niceties to touch Charny's general reputation as a knight.

A more significant argument could rest on the attitude of the French king. He must have approved Charny's plan in advance. Thus in his eyes Charny, far from being compromised, was evidently considered ever more worthy. Philippe VI died while Charny was a captive in London, but his successor, Jean II, contributed heavily toward Charny's ransom in July 1351.[22] As we will see, he also chose Charny unhesitatingly as a member of the new chivalric order he founded in the following year. He apparently even commissioned him to write the series of works intended to set the moral tone of this new royal order. Charny was scarcely under a cloud in France. Perhaps most fighting men of the time would simply have thought that Charny played the game by a hard set of rules, and when he lost temporarily, endured Edward's taunting rebuke in stoic silence as the only practical response.

In the summer of 1351 Charny was back in the war in France. He fought at Ardres in June; in July he took part in negotiations between the King of France and the Count of Flanders; in September he attended the negotiations that prolonged the Anglo-French truce.

His new responsibilities were indicated by the sonorous title of "Captain General of the Wars of Picardie and the Frontiers of Normandy." Watching the danger point of Calais he apparently ambushed an English force of several hundred men setting out on a raid, killing or capturing all of them.[23] Such attention to his duties did not deter him from settling a personal score. Whether or not he had suffered any doubts about his attempt at Calais, he had no doubts that Aimery had betrayed him and should be dealt with accordingly. Aimery was now living in a fortified dwelling given to him by Edward III, who had nonetheless removed him from any position at Calais. Good service must be rewarded, but trust apparently went only so far. Aimery, if we can believe Froissart, was living a joyful life with an English mistress named Marguerite. Charny decided on a night raid, which this time was a complete success. He surprised Aimery—Froissart insists he was in bed with Marguerite, who with distressing pragmatism soon took up with a French squire—and led him back to his base at St. Omer. There he decapitated the Lombard, quartered his body, and displayed it at the town gates. To show that all this was a private matter and not a part of the business of war, prohibited for a time by the current truce, Charny took possession only of Aimery himself, not his castle.[24]

Aimery de Pavia was, in Charny's eyes, a traitor in the broad contemporary sense (encountered often in medieval literature) of faithlessness to sworn word. This is disloyalty. What Charny would say about the loyalty Aimery owed to Edward III remains unknowable. But Charny came to the same judgment of disloyalty in the case of Hugues de Belconroy, the French commander of the castle of Guines, who had delivered his fortress to the English for a sum of money. Here was a traitor in the emerging political sense of disloyalty to the king of France. When Belconroy was captured and turned over to Charny at St. Omer, Charny had the man put to death. Belconroy had, of course, done precisely what Charny had expected Aimery to do.[25] Perhaps Charny would not have objected had the English king similarly executed Aimery, if he had kept to his bargain, delivered Calais to the French, and later had the misfortune of being captured by his English lords. Unfaithful to his sworn agreement with Charny, Aimery deserved death; Belconroy, unfaithful to his king, likewise deserved death. Charny might have felt surprise at any sense of moral ambiguity on our part. Did not both the castle of Guines and the castle and town of Calais rightfully belong to the king of France?

In January 1352, this king was breathing life into a plan that had lived only in his imagination since 1344, when he was simply duke of Normandy and heir to the throne. Jean II wanted to create a company of knights that could stand as the premier order of chivalry in the Christian West. His noble Company of the Star would, he hoped, outshine even Edward's royal chivalric order announced only a few months previous (Edward's plan would later result in the Order of the Garter).[26] The French royal order, dedicated to the Blessed Virgin, was to be served by an ecclesiastical college that would provide divine service and pray for the knightly conduct of the members. The company was to meet twice annually in the royal manor of Saint-Ouen, embellished for its new role with significant renovations as well as the new name of the Noble Maison. If he could have enrolled 500 members as planned, this order would have encompassed between an eighth and a fifth of all the knights in the realm.

In fact, far from dominating the world of fourteenth-century chivalry, the Company of the Star crumbled swiftly and completely under the hammer blows of defeat on the battlefield and the corrosion of internecine strife. Perhaps more than eighty members died in a battle described by Froissart (apparently the battle of Mauron in Brittany in August 1352). The casualty rate may well have resulted from an oath taken by the members that they would not flee a battle. After the yet more disastrous defeat of French chivalry and the capture of King Jean himself at Poitiers in 1356, the order was virtually dead.

But in the heady days of its founding the Company of the Star, could consider themselves elevated to the pinnacle of the chivalric world. Indeed, as Jonathon Bolton suggests, "Charny seems to have been the very model of the sort of knighthood that Jean was attempting to promote when he founded the Company of the Star, and it is very probable that Charny composed all three of his works on chivalry at Jean's request."[27]

The ultimate chivalric honor for Charny, however, has yet to be mentioned. In March 1347, and again in June 1355, Jean II named him the bearer or keeper of the oriflamme,[28] the sacred banner of the king of France. This banner was raised boldly in the front ranks of his major battles. Contemporary opinion held that the keeper must be "the most worthy and the most adept warrior" (le plus preudomme et plus preux es armes), that the king's choice must fall on "a knight noble in intention and deed, unwavering, virtuous, loyal, adept, and chivalrous, one who fears and loves God (ung chevalier noble en couraige et en fais, constant et vertueulx, loyal, preux, et chevalereux et qui doubte et ayme Dieu)". The oriflamme, a tasseled square or rectangle of red silk ending in a number of small streamers, was attached in battle to a gilded lance. In peacetime it was reverently deposited in the monastery at St. Denis. Periodically the kings of France brought it forth for war in an elaborate liturgy involving masses, relics, and benedictions. Immersed in this atmosphere of candlelight and incense, the guardian of the oriflamme, kneeling with head bared, took the following oath, said out to him by the Abbot of St. Denis:

You swear and promise on the precious, sacred body of Jesus Christ present here and on the bodies of Monsigneur Saint Denis and his fellows which are here, that you will loyally in person hold and keep the oriflamme of our lord king, who is here, to his honor and profit and that of his realm, and not abandon it for fear of death or whatever else may happen, and you will do your duty everywhere as a good and loyal knight must toward his sovereign and proper lord.

After this oath the king himself raised the bearer to his feet and kissed him on the mouth. The bearer then genuflected before the potent relics and took the sacred banner in his joined hands; he raised it aloft for all to see. The lords and barons present were permitted to kiss (*embrasser*) the oriflamme "as a relic and worthy thing." If the banner was not already attached to its lance, the king draped it dramatically around the shoulders of its bearer for the recessional. On the battlefield at Poitiers in the early autumn of 1356, Geoffroi de Charny unfailingly met the conditions of his solemn oath as keeper of the oriflamme.

The climactic battle was provoked by a renewed English invasion. As part of an ambitious three-pronged attack, Edward the Black Prince had led an Anglo-Gascon force from Bordeaux into central France. In fact, the Black Prince soon found himself pursued (slowed down by dragging along a vast load of booty) by a much larger French host commanded by Jean II in person. So certain of victory was the French king that he brushed aside the peace negotiations of two cardinals and insisted on battle. The English likewise brushed aside the classic chivalric suggestion of Charny that the conflict be settled by one hundred chosen champions on each side, to limit the bloodshed.[29] It was a grand gesture and probably was appreciated as such.

On September 19 near Poitiers the French suffered one of their worst military disasters of the Middle Ages. A charge of elite French knights failed to break through improvised English defense lines, and the battle became a confused series of piecemeal actions. King Jean took his stand at the center of the most desperate fighting, with Charny close at hand. Froissart's words picture the action vividly:

There Sir Geoffroy de Charny fought gallantly near the King. The whole press and cry of battle were upon him because he was carrying the King's sovereign banner [the oriflamme]. He also had before him on the field his own banner, gules, three escutcheons argent [three silver shields on a red background]. So many English and Gascons came around him from all sides that they cracked open the King's battle formation and smashed it; there were so many English and Gascons that at least five of these men-at-arms attacked one [French] gentleman. Sir Geoffroy de

Charny was killed with the banner of France in his hands, and the French banners fell to the earth.[30]

Before he was killed, Charny had cut down the first man to lay a hand on the bridle of Jean's horse, but now the king was forced to yield to enemies who surrounded him shouting, "Give yourself up! Give yourself up!"[31]

The consequences of this battle can be read at length in the tumultuous history of France in the later fourteenth century. But the conclusion to Charny's own story is quickly told. His body was first buried at Poitiers, at the house of the Grey Friars, but was taken from Poitiers to Paris at royal expense and given formal reburial in 1370 in the church of the Celestines, a site frequently used by the crown for the burials of royal servants. Since Charny's son, the second Geoffroi, died without heirs in 1398, the Charny line ended with him.[32]

Told in this way, the story of Charny's life takes on a bleak cast. Vigorous and valiant as he may have been, he was captured twice, went on a useless crusade, failed to secure Calais for his king, and was hacked to death in the great set-piece battle for which he had presumably longed all his life. Yet such a summary would miss much that he and his contemporaries considered crucially important. He had obviously fought valiantly in one encounter after another. He was vastly admired by his contemporaries and his actions won enthusiastic words of praise from chroniclers on both sides of the Channel. To Froissart, Charny was "the most worthy and valiant of them all."[33] To the English chronicler Geoffrey le Baker, he was "a knight more skilled in military matters than any other Frenchman, so that his fame was widespread and who also, through long practice of arms and by a lively, wise character, was until his death . . . chief counselor of young French knights."[34] And when we turn to the ideals he presents in his writing we find that he lived the sort of life he most valued, dying in the manner most fitting his strong sense of vocation. Moreover, through the window of his words, we modern readers can get a new glimpse into the lay aristocratic mind of his age. Charny could lay claim to the title of theoretician of chivalry in fourteenth-century France, one of its most congenial homes.

The Revitalization of Chivalry

What does it mean to say Geoffroi de Charny was the author of the *Book of Chivalry*? Authorship need not imply penmanship. That is, we should probably not picture Charny's well-developed frame bent over a writing desk, dipping quill into inkwell. Given increasing literacy and improved noble education we can be certain that Charny could read French and possibly some Latin. These changing cultural conditions may indicate Charny could also write; but the likelihood is that he relied on a scribe, as most members of the privileged social orders did. We might justly picture Charny not only dictating to a scribe, but perhaps pacing back and forth to put his characteristic vigor to work in the service of composition. Certainly his text reveals that he exclaimed an occasional "He! Dieu!" (Ah! God!) to emphasize a point he felt with particular keenness. The issue then is how well he could organize his thoughts and express his ideas formally, whoever held the pen.

Although Charny wrote three treatises, the *Book of Chivalry* is clearly his major work. He also wrote *Questions concerning the Joust, Tournament, and War*,[35] a long series of intricate questions on chivalric practice. These appear without answers and were probably meant to be debated by the members of the Company of the Star. There is also a *Livre Charny*,[36] "the Charny Book," a verse work on the manner of life and the qualities demanded by chivalry; but it is a less fully developed work than the *Book of Chivalry* presented here. This *Book of Chivalry*, and indeed each of his books, shows us a man who could organize a large-scale argument as well as direct a systematic siege or a thunderous cavalry charge. Like a mass of armed horsemen with the blood up, his sheer momentum sometimes leads him astray. He then corrects direction and gets back on course. It is important to sense his successive objectives, all planned to bring ultimate victory for his ideals. His own wordiness is ironically the enemy. Charny will never stop with one term when three would do. Perhaps this comes from a man of great energy dictating, arms cutting through the air like sword strokes. No doubt the wordiness comes not only from the French vernacular, but from strong belief in the ideology he presents. The urge to adorn and amplify his prose is irresistible to him. Charny thinks in long sentences and complete thoughts—often even in whole paragraphs. He must be read that way. His book is better understood if read out loud and dramatically, ideally with a flagon of wine at the ready.

In short, this is a man with ideas whose words tumble forth in his passion for his vocation. He speaks for the group, for the entire *ordo* (the divinely ordained socio-professional body) of chivalry that has come into existence over the previous two centuries. As we will see, the particular circumstances of his age leave their mark on what he says; yet we read

Charny because he speaks for knighthood with force, rather than for mid-fourteenth-century French knighthood alone. Any originality that he shows never reduces his book to the particular or the idiosyncratic.

Charny's *Book of Chivalry* is thus a gold mine because it reveals where a thoughtful model knight stands in the vigorous medieval debate over chivalry. By his time that debate was more than two centuries old. The motivating force behind it is not far to seek: so powerful a force as chivalry understandably attracted many attempts at direction and control. The ethos of the laymen who held the swords was of much concern in a society working to find new forms of order. Clerics, intellectuals, and eventually knights themselves joined the fray. They all wanted to fit the highly necessary but potentially disruptive force represented by the knights into their ideal view of that society.

There were those with doubts that this goal could actually be reached. Bernard of Clairvaux (1090–1153), the powerful voice of monasticism, had breathed the scorching fire of his critiques on the general body of knighthood. He reserved his honeyed praise for the crusading order of monk-knights only, the Knights Templar.[37] The great mass of knights was obviously rushing to perdition. The few sanctified monk/knights won the great abbot's praise as ideal warriors who fought only the pagan enemy and avoided the pitfalls of mere earthly chivalry. The great body of knights, who blindly followed earthly chivalry, made prowess and tourneying laudable ends in themselves; they remained strangers to the great virtue of chastity. Only the "new knighthood" of the Temple, as he wrote in a treatise sent to the master of the new order, "ceaselessly wages a twofold war both against flesh and blood and against a spiritual army of evil in the heavens. . . . What a glory to return in victory from such a battle! How blessed to die there as a martyr!" The great mass of non-Templar knights, by contrast, are still mired in "worldly knighthood, or rather knavery, as I should call it." Thinking of the generality of knighthood Bernard thunders blandishments in his best style:

What then, O knights, is this monstrous error and what this unbearable urge which bids you fight with such pomp and labor, and all to no purpose except death and sin? You cover your horses with silk, and plume your armor with I know not what sort of rags; you paint your shield and your saddles; you adorn your bits and spurs with gold and silver and precious stones, and then in all this glory you rush to your ruin with fearful wrath and fearless folly.[38]

Though he later preached the Second Crusade, thus valorizing at least all crusaders rather than Templars alone, he could never fully accept knighthood as it existed in the world outside his monastic walls. To ensure salvation, a knight should ideally join the Templars, die heroically on crusade, or get to a monastery and convert to the religious (i.e., the monastic) life swiftly.

Chrétien de Troyes, famed as the father of chivalric romance, in the late twelfth century wrote magisterial works in joyous praise of knighthood. He loved elite and colorful display, carried out in courtly style. Yet even he saw chivalric life warts and all and sought significant reform. In his sophisticated romance *Yvain, the Knight with the Lion*, for example, he presents the transformation of a knight into his ideal. A young hero who begins with the common knightly values (including pride, vainglory, and revenge for shamed kindred) learns to use his great capacity in arms for socially useful purposes.

Early in the thirteenth century the great cycle of prose romances known as the Lancelot-Grail or Vulgate Cycle shows the debate continuing in full vigor.[39] The earliest text in this cycle (The *Lancelot*) praises the illicit and secret love of Lancelot and Guinevere. A later text in the same cycle (The *Quest for the Holy Grail*) can be read as the negation of the *Lancelot*. It seems to be almost an anti-romance. Chivalry becomes an allegory for the quest of the spiritual life, a high goal that can be achieved by three extraordinary men only out of all the Round Table brotherhood. The final text (the *Death of King Arthur*) narrates the collapse of this greatest chivalric fellowship ever imagined, but simultaneously documents the spiritual ascent of Lancelot as a just warrior in the world who ends his life as a spiritual recluse. In short, on large issues the romances in this cycle take differing points of view. On scores of smaller, particular points, moreover, this Vulgate Cycle, like the Bible for which it has been named, can again yield differing interpretations. Authors debate even such technical questions as whether a mounted man can legitimately attack an unhorsed opponent. Can several men honorably fight against one?

In the vast body of chivalric texts, in other words, different points of view contend on issues large and small. We are reminded that chivalry played a crucial role in society, provoking great efforts to direct its energies. Various writers wanted to shape it along lines of their choosing. Far too many works entered this debate even for mention here.

As a general rule, however, we can say that most works are in broad terms more prescriptive than descriptive. In other words, they prescribe ideal behavior for the knights. Their clerical authors are setting forth not what chivalry is in the world around them, but what they would like it to be in order to fit the knights into the Christian society under construction. Useful as they are, such works cannot match Charny's text in closeness to actual knighthood. Granted, he too has prescriptive ideals. Yet he is a strenuous knight writing highly practical advice in a time of crisis for French chivalry. The *Book of Chivalry* stays close to the real world in which it was written. Charny's engagement with his profession, the audience for whom he wrote, the times in which he wrote—all combine to keep his book close to actual, historical knighthood.

We can be fairly certain that Charny wrote his books in 1350–51 for the Company of the Star, the new chivalric order of his king, Jean II. He could well have put to good use the enforced leisure of temporary captivity in England during these years after the disastrous attempt to secure Calais. A general reform of French governance was underway, chivalric reform was one component of that reform, and this royal order of knights was to be the centerpiece of chivalric revival. France was in crisis and her knighthood was critically important to recovery. The problem was most plainly the repeated defeat of French arms. English armies seemed to strike at will and move where they wanted, leaving behind them a trail of looted and charred villages. French arms had not done well in trying to stop them with set-piece battles. On the sea at Sluys in 1340, and in the long awaited land battle at Crécy in 1346, French men-at-arms had been beaten badly. Their English foes held Calais, a base for future operations and irritating raids. Clearly the glittering ranks of knights led by the kings of France were unable to provide for defense. They were failing at the very function on which so much of their claim to honor and their enjoyment of dominance and wealth finally rested. Each raid by the English and their allies underscored the point.

Within France itself there was no shortage of critics who pointed accusingly to these failures. Bitter satires attacked the knights and the nobles in general, accusing them of cowardice, immorality and greed. As the defense of the kingdom crumbled, critics cried out that the elite collected ever larger sums of money which they spent frivolously. Moreover, the nobles risked the wrath of God by a shameful and costly display of vanity in the outrageous clothing they now sported. The Carmelite friar, Jean de Venette, who seems to have been closely in touch with popular opinion, pointedly worried that such immoral men would run in the face of the enemy. He also wanted to follow the money supposedly spent on defense. As he wrote in 1346,

Officials were being enriched, the king impoverished. Money was contributed to many nobles and knights that they might aid and defend their land and kingdom, but it was all spent for the useless practices of pleasure, such as dice and other unseemly games.[40]

Just before giving an account of the disastrous battle of Poitiers, he charged that "the luxury and dissoluteness of many of the nobles and the knights became still more deeply rooted." Reminding his readers of knightly dress already immoral by becoming scanty and form-fitting, he now denounced the fashion to "adorn themselves from head to foot with gems and precious stones." The knights were buying up jewels with such enthusiasm that prices shot up dramatically in Paris. Jean pours scorn on them:

By night they devoted themselves immoderately to the pleasures of the flesh or to games of dice; by day, to ball or tennis. Wherefore the common people had reason to lament, and did lament greatly, that the taxes levied on them for the war were uselessly spent on such sports and converted to such uses.[41]

Jean de Venette was scarcely alone. Another chronicler was certain that God was punishing the nobility of France for their pride, greed, and indecency of dress[42]. The flower of French chivalry had been cut down on the battlefield at Crécy in punishment for these very sins. Yet another chronicler denounced the nobles for their long beards and tunics so short they displayed their backsides, "which caused in the general populace a considerable derision." This author at once connects such morals with a tendency to flee in the face of the enemy.[43] After the battle of Poitiers the Benedictine monk Francis Beaumont would declare French chivalry a subject for satire; its soft cowardice painfully undercut its pride; the knights who had run like rabbits, leaving their brave king to be captured, had elevated pleasure and luxury above discipline and military art, in the process bringing the ruin of the French state.[44]

Perhaps the atmosphere had darkened in Charny's early youth as the King of France, Philippe le Bel, brought down the venerable Order of the Knights of the Temple, charging these model monk-knights with shocking immorality and heresy and arresting nearly 2,000 brothers. Charny, however, never mentions the Templars and there is no evidence connecting him to them, despite some wild modern speculation. He does, we will see, talk tirelessly about that most essential chivalric trait, prowess. The crisis at its most basic level stemmed from the serious and repeated defeats of

French knighthood; they failed to show the needed prowess. Charny skillfully carried out the reformer's balancing act. Of course he gave free rein to his inclination to praise chivalry to the skies. He also had to point the finger of blame without calling too much attention to the tarnish and corrosion (seen all too clearly by other critics, outside the charmed circle). Thus he identified problems and urged reforms to realize the potential of chivalry and blunt the criticisms voiced against it. Prowess had to be revitalized first.

There was another crucial problem for which a reformed chivalry could provide a solution. Unable to provide for defense, French chivalry likewise proved unable to maintain unity within the ranks of the powerful. As they failed to demonstrate the great virtue of prowess, their loyalty began to disintegrate as well. Here was a second major chivalric virtue in decline. Loyalty required not only adherence to their king, but to the working ideals of their *ordo*. The ideals of chivalry would give steadfastness and cohesion to their essential profession. An entire set of issues that might be individually labeled political or military or social therefore converged. The Valois kings who had succeeded the senior line of the Capetian dynasty in 1328 feared, with good reason, that their hold on the crown was somewhat shaky. A certain level of quarreling between the king and some great lords was only to be expected. But the issue began to look much more serious toward the mid-fourteenth century. Some great French lords scandalously defected to the English (Robert d'Artois and Geoffroi de Harcourt). The king ordered the summary execution of his constable (Raoul, Count of Eu). Even another member of the royal family (Charles of Evreux and Navarre) showed flickering ambitions to take the throne for himself. Any reasonably acute observer would have feared the factionalism that would, in time, make the Hundred Years War a veritable civil war in France. Many observers began to raise doubts whether the high privilege of the knights was earned by virtuous performance and steady loyalty.

Jean II's clear goal was to right the wrongs before it was too late. He wanted Charny's treatises to be read and discussed by the members of the Company of the Star. It would be a sizeable group of readers or listeners. The king's plan called for membership in the order to reach 500 men, more than 150 of whom were to be simple bachelors; possibly men of this rank were to form the majority. Each year, as the king announced, three princes, three bannerets, and three bachelors would sit at a Table of Honor. Reform was to reach all layers of those who bore arms; defeat was to be turned into victory, moral decay into discipline. King Jean voiced his hope, even as he cautiously identified the problem, in his letters (October, 1342) endowing his new royal chivalric order:

Jean by the Grace of God King of France. . . . Among the other preoccupations of our mind, we have many times asked ourself with all the energy of reflection, by what means the knighthood of our realm has, from ancient times, sent forth into the whole world such a burst of probity, and has been crowned with so lively an aureole of valiance and honour; so well that our ancestors the Kings of France, thanks to the powerful intervention of heaven and to the faithful devotion of this knighthood, which has bestowed upon them the sincere and unanimous concourse of its arms, have always triumphed over all the rebels whom they have wished to reduce; that they have been able, with the aid of divine favour, to restore to the pure paths of the Catholic Faith the numberless victims that the perfidious Enemy of the human race, through ruse and artifice, had made to err against the true faith; and finally that they had established in the realm a peace and security so profound that, after many long centuries, some of the members of this order, unaccustomed to arms and deprived of exercises, or for some other cause unknown to us, have immoderately plunged themselves into the idleness and vanity of the age, to the contempt of honour, alas, and of their good renown, to diminish their gaiety of heart in exchange for the comfort of their persons. For this reason we, mindful of former times, of the honourable and constant prowess of the aforesaid liegemen, who brought forth so many victorious, virtuous, and fortunate works, have taken it to heart to recall these same liegemen, present and future, to a perfect union, to the end that in this intimate unity they will breathe nothing but honour and glory, renouncing the frivolities of inaction, and will, through respect for the prestige of the nobility and knighthood, restore to our epoch the lustre of their ancient renown and of their illustrious company, and that after they have brought about the reflowering of the honour of knighthood through the protection of divine goodness, a tranquil peace will be reborn for our reign and our subjects, and the praises of their virtue will be published everywhere. Therefore, in expectation of these benefits and of many others, we . . . have founded [the Company of the Star and its college of clerics]. And we have firm confidence that with the intercession of the said most glorious Virgin Mary for us and our faithful subjects, the Lord Jesus Christ will mercifully pour out his grace upon the knights of the aforesaid company or association, with the result that the same knights, eager for honour and glory in the exercise of arms, shall bear themselves with such concord and valiance, that the flower of chivalry, which for a time and for the reasons mentioned had faded into the shadows, shall blossom in our realm, and shine resplendent in a perfect harmony to the honour and glory of the kingdom and of our faithful subjects.[45]

It is worth noting that one clause in the letter notifying members of the Company of their election specifies that any member who shamefully fled from a battle would be expelled from the order until he had cleared his name.

All the familiar themes are here. Chivalry has been the grand force for good, the strong arm of true faith, favored by God, the agency of defense, the guarantor of good and peaceful governance, the procurer of glorious victories. But the flower of chivalry has faded under dark shadows cast by weakness and defeat. Only vigorous reform can restore a knighthood that will throw off sloth and immorality and be "eager for honour and glory in the exercise of arms." The anxious king and the honored knight who carried his banner and wrote as theoretician of chivalry saw the same issues and spoke to them in the same language.

Prowess and Honor

Two contexts thus inform Charny's *Book of Chivalry*. On the one hand he stands within a long tradition of debate over the place of knighthood in medieval society. On the other hand he is writing about French knighthood in an era of crisis and sharp criticism. His response—so important to him and so useful to us—is to urge a return to the basics, to emphasize the core values of his profession. All will be well if the men who bear arms understand the two principle themes he advances. First: prowess is the essential chivalric trait and leads to honor, the highest human good. Second: this prowess is the gift of God, requiring ceaseless thankfulness.

The emphasis on prowess will at once strike any reader of Charny's work. In the opening pages of his treatise Charny carefully lays out a scale of knightly deeds, drawing on the categories of prowess familiar to his audience through military contracts: the joust, the tournament, and war.[46] All men-at-arms are honorable, he insists, as are all acts of prowess: "I maintain," Charny says tersely, "that there are no small feats of arms" (Section 3). But the honor of those who primarily joust (one knight against another) will not match that of the men who engage in the tourney, where many knights contend on each side. The tourneyers must, in turn, yield pride of place to those who engage in actual war. The reason for this scale is the increasing requirement of prowess: the tourney, of course, involves jousting, but it also includes the dangerous free-for-all of the *mêlée*. As war encompasses all the forms of combat, it brings the highest honor. War occupies the greatest space in another of Charny's treatises, the *Questions* (*Demandes*), where Charny poses 20 questions concerning

joust, 21 on *mêlée*, and 93 on war. In effect, Charny moves his reader along an upward scale of prowess from the two types of deeds of arms in peacetime to the more comprehensive, strenuous, and risky deeds of arms in war. Repeatedly Charny states this principle in lapidary form "he who does more is worth more" (*qui plus fait, mieux vault*).

This emphasis on prowess firmly links Charny to the ideals for knighthood we can find in other sources close to real life knights. For prowess involved the entire cluster of warrior virtues: great strength, hardiness, and skill in using arms on horseback or on foot as well as the courage and determination that must inform success at arms. This potent set of qualities and abilities animates much of the literature of chivalry.[47]

Moreover, success at arms brings honor, the most desired human trait in medieval lay society. As Froissart observed, "As firewood cannot burn without flame, neither can a gentleman achieve perfect honor nor worldly renown without prowess" (Si comme la busce ne poet ardoir sans feu, ne poet li gentilz homs venir a parfait honneur ne a la glore dou monde sans proece).[48] Honor to a modern person may mean a rather general sense of being a decent man or woman—keeping one's word, never cheating. Indeed, chivalry conveys this quality (under the label of loyalty) in the Middle Ages. Then—and throughout much of early history, however—honor

obviously conveys a much more assertive and even prickly sense. Honor is
best won at someone else's expense through force; it is the fruit of a highly
physical process. The great deeds to which Charny regularly refers involve
edged weaponry. He is not, of course, praising men of mere brutality, nor
berserkers wiping foam from their quaking lips. Such characteristics would
scarcely form the man of worth he upholds as the ideal. Yet we would
equally miss the point if we imagined prowess as a purely mental or emo-
tional quality, operating in a world unstained by blood, sweat and tears.
The increasing physicality of combat, the muscular energy and the rising
bodily risks entailed in joust, tourney and war are precisely what Charny
values.

Any modern reader, and certainly any modern military historian, may
wonder at this emphasis on personal prowess. Why does Charny not out-
line battlefield tactics, let alone some broader concept of strategy to revi-
talize the French military? The reflexive modern answer is likely to assert
that medieval knights thought little and charged often, that there truly
was no medieval science of warfare. In fact, as John Gillingham has demonstrated from sound evidence, great twelfth-century knights such as
Richard I and William Marshal practiced a policy emphasizing military
objectives over individual display.[49] Their wars were based on administrative effectiveness and involved strategies of ravaging enemy territory; their
leadership was scarcely confined to a simple-minded search for dramatic
and risky battlefield confrontations. Moreover they were open about this
preference. When Marshal advised Henry II to fool the French by pretend-
ing to disband his forces and then secretly assembling them for a swift
campaign of ravaging, the English king praised William's advice as "most
courteous" (*molt corteis*).[50] Looking at the generations between Marshal
and Charny, no one could doubt that administrative efficiency supporting
warfare continued to grow or that commanders understood that ravaging
enemy territory was the best option when fighting set-piece battles against
a powerful host was too dangerous. Clifford Rogers has commented on a
treatise produced for the French crown in 1300 tellingly entitled "The
Doctrine of Successful Expeditions and Shortened Wars." This treatise by
Pierre Dubois advocated less attention to sieges of walled strongholds in
favor of the devastation of villages, countryside and crops.[51] Ironically, the
success of the English along just these lines could soon be traced in their
scorched progress through the kingdom of France. Their evident success
must have burned itself into Charny's consciousness as well. Why, then, in

so practical a treatise as the *Book of Chivalry* does he not suggest specific tactical and strategic responses?

If we could interview Charny we might find him somewhat puzzled at the stark alternatives implied in our questions. Of course warfare is a matter of manoeuver, he might say; of course you ravage your enemies' territory whenever possible and deceive him when you can. He might elaborate for us some bold plans for an invasion of the England he actually saw only as a prisoner. He could point to sections of his text enjoining young knights to learn all they can about the best techniques of campaigning (e.g., Section 17). But these are lessons to be learned only in the field, from the best practitioners, not from a book, not even from his book. The granite foundation on which all such campaigning rests, he might tell us with waning patience, is that complex of military virtues he would sum up as prowess. This is the fit subject for his book. In formal writing for the royal chivalric order, why belabor details of military practice on which all seasoned warriors broadly agreed? The clear need is for French knighthood to hear again the clarion call of chivalry, to give up the soft life and be willing to undertake the pains and privations of knighthood. Perhaps that would mean besieging some stronghold through endless rainy days on bad rations. It just might bring that glorious apotheosis of prowess, a full-blown battle. In either case it is a set of personal qualities that Charny wants his knights to have and that he thinks absolutely necessary. He is preaching a kind of military morality with prowess as its center. As he writes, "anyone who wants to attain this high honor, if he retains his physical health and lives for long enough, cannot and should not be excused from achieving it" (Section 19); "but no one should or can excuse himself from being a man of worth and loyal, if he has the will" (Section 24).

This theme runs through the entire treatise. With few exceptions, all other qualities or actions are judged by their capacity to encourage and increase prowess. This is the yardstick by which all else is measured. Repeatedly, Charny decries the fear of mere death, for example. Those afraid to die will not boldly risk all, sword in hand. The true warrior always expects that one day he will feel a mortal wound from sword stroke or lance thrust. He cannot regret the blow. If he has lived appropriately he can die appropriately.

The chivalric life obviously cannot be focused on bodily comfort. Charny's scathing denunciations of soft beds, sleeping late, insistence on just the right foods would do credit to an uncompromising monastic reformer. His goal, of course, is a martial rather than a spiritual result—to encourage and preserve bodily discipline for the all-important exercise of prowess.

This emphasis on prowess even explains why we find him shuddering at the sight of current male fashions in clothing. The trend had apparently begun among valets and artisans and through young serving men made its way up the social hierarchy into noble society. He agrees wholeheartedly with the clerical moralists who object to clothing so shameful that the wearer should be embarrassed to appear in it. Men who wear clothing molded to reveal the body and who with disgusting vanity cover their clothing with rich ornament can only have forgotten shame, and those who have forgotten shame have forgotten honor as well. It is only appropriate for women to adorn their bodies with jewels, he insists, because they lack the opportunity to win gilded honor through prowess. For men the matter necessarily stands otherwise.

The appearance of ladies brings us to the most striking case of the preeminence of prowess yet to be mentioned. We are accustomed to thinking of ladies and love as soon as we hear the words "knights and chivalry." In some academic circles chivalry has come almost to be considered synonymous with formal doctrines of Courtly Love. The *Book of Chivalry* is a good corrective to such views. Ladies and the love they inspire are truly important to Charny. We will want to think soon about the issues of sexual morality raised by gender relationships. We will see that Charny has thoughts about how knights should manage love affairs. But for the present we must note that the significance of females in elite society arises in his view from their capacity to incite and inspire men to do great deeds of prowess. These deeds will—at least so all male chivalric writers assert—win their hearts utterly. Charny gives an unforgettable picture (in Section 20) of the lady whose heart swells with pride as her lover enters the hall and is recognized as a valiant knight, while the lady whose lover has shown no prowess feels downcast as he enters, only to be universally ignored.

The Knight and Piety

After even a few pages of his book a reader will be convinced that Charny's thought is steeped in piety. His tone is insistently religious, at times even puritanical. His providential view is almost a mental reflex. He insists again and again that whatever happens in the world is the will of God. One must therefore take reverses patiently and accept honors humbly. The lasting rewards in life are not randomly handed out. Fortune may seem for a time a rogue force, but it has no permanent power. God will distribute the real rewards to His warriors for their good deeds.

An important feature is Charny's appropriation of religious ideas and language. For example, Charny borrows traditional medieval Christian denigration of the body in contrast to the immortal soul. He speaks of "this puny body that lives only the space of an hour." This phrase might sound strange in the mouth of a knight much given to the praise of prowess, the ultimate display of bodily strength. But Charny is writing of the slothful and the timid, who do not make the most of their bodies, fearing to risk them in the all-important quest for honor. A body used well gains honor which (like the soul), is immortal.

In fact for Charny there is a parallel between pairs of contrasting ideas in chivalry and in religion. The religious contrast of body and soul is paralleled by the knightly contrast of worldly possessions or worldly comforts and all-important honor. That is, mere possessions or comforts are to chivalry what the mere body is to religion. Honor in chivalry is like the soul in religion. Significantly, in discussing the ancient Jewish hero Judas Maccabeus as the ideal knight Charny emphasizes the two great gifts God granted him: earthly honor and eternal salvation. In Charny's mind the honor of the body and the salvation of the soul stand together. However Christian their form in his book, such ideas reveal the age-old belief of warriors that daring and hardship are rewarded by bliss; Geoffroi expected his heavenly reward with the Lord of Hosts as ardently as any Viking anticipated Valhalla.

Just as striking is Charny's appropriation of the concept of righteous suffering or even martyrdom. This was one of the most powerful sets of ideas in medieval Christianity. It is important to Charny to say how hard it is to be a knight, how hard to give up the ease he condemns, to work the body constantly and risk it in battle. Striving to explain, he emphasizes the suffering a good knight willingly undergoes; he states in another of his books, the *Livre Charny*, that knights carry heavier loads than beasts of burden. Suffering and the risk of violent death in a good cause connect with religious ideas, perhaps even (distantly if not explicitly) with the sacrifice and violent death of Christ.

It seems significant, then, that in his *Book of Chivalry* he asserts that knights suffer more than the clergy: "the good order of knighthood . . . should be considered the most rigorous order of all, especially for those who uphold it well and conduct themselves in a way in keeping with the purpose for which the order was established." Considering the "hard-ships, pains, discomforts, fears, perils, broken bones, and wounds which the good knights . . . have to suffer frequently, there is no religious order in which as much is suffered" (Section 40). In his verse treatise on chiv-alry, Charny speaks with considerable realism and frankness about the knight's suffering in battle: arrows and lances rain down on him; he sees his friends' bodies sprawled on the ground all around him; he is well-mounted and could escape, but to flee would be a loss of honor. "Is he not a great martyr," Charny asks rhetorically, "who puts himself to such work?"[52]

The powerful language of martyrdom allows Charny to accomplish several important goals at once. He vents feelings about the weariness of constant campaigning that would otherwise sound like mere complaining. He expresses what must have been a genuine, if usually unspoken, fear on the part of men who regularly faced other men armed with edged weap-ons. He casts a mantle of righteousness over the knightly vocation. Its practitioners and others should see it, for all its violence, as pleasing in the eyes of God. In fact, he uses the suffering of knights inversely to elevate their status.

The piety that led Charny to appropriate religious language for his discussion of chivalry left fascinating traces beyond the pages of his book.[53] As early as 1343, he planned to found a church on his estate at Lirey. Five clerics would serve the chapel, praying and saying masses continuously for Charny and his family and for the king and the royal family. Over the remaining years of his life, Charny sent to the papal court a number of requests for himself and his church. He obtained the right to have a porta-ble altar, to receive from his confessor a plenary indulgence "in articulo mortis" (i.e., just before death), to hear a first mass of the day before sunrise, to have a family cemetery next to his church at Lirey, and to have his body divided into parts for burial in separate locations. This aristocratic religious fashion stimulated beneficial prayers from more than one group of clerics.

To modern eyes, however, perhaps the most intriguing indication of Charny's piety comes from his ownership of the piece of linen cloth known today as the Shroud of Turin. This remarkable cloth, reverently regarded by some as the actual burial wrapping of Christ, seems to bear an imprint from the front and back of his crucified body. Charny has long been recog-nized as the first historical owner of the Shroud though its date remains a matter of controversy. Modern scientific efforts to date the Shroud allow at least a speculation that Charny may have been its original owner. Controlled radiocarbon tests of a sample from the Shroud, conducted at several laboratories in the late 1980s, dated the cloth to 1260–1390 ("with at least 95 percent confidence")—the likelihood of manufacture being, of course, most pronounced in the middle of this range of years centering on 1325.[54] These tests indicate that the Shroud was made in Charny's lifetime. Yet controversy, scientific and religious, continues. Some have suggested the Shroud dates from the seventh century.[55] Those who believe the Shroud to be an authentic relic from the lifetime of Christ, insist that material accumulating on the Shroud from later centuries have given false results to the scientific dating. This claim has been scientifically disputed as obviously insufficient to redate the Shroud to the first century A.D. Another claim, currently beyond present capacity for testing, holds that bacterial and fungal infestation has produced a bioplastic coating on the fibers of the Shroud, altering the range of dates suggested.[56]

Although virtually no aspect of the history of the Shroud has escaped controversy, Charny's involvement is slightly less entangled than others. For our purposes the Shroud—whatever its date—simply but effectively complements the picture of pronounced religiosity displayed in Charny's writing. Nonetheless his ownership raises interesting questions that cannot be brushed aside altogether. Exactly how and when the Shroud came into Charny's possession remains tantalizingly unknown. Charny's church at Lirey eventually housed the Shroud, but in the repeated papal grants Charny secured for this chapel he makes no mention of the Shroud whatsoever. In fact, only a few thin, if strong, strands of evidence convincingly link Charny to the Shroud.

Shortly after Charny's death, a papal letter referred to the Shroud which had been "generously given to him (*liberaliter sibi oblatam*)". In a memorandum sent to the papal court, probably in early 1390, the bishop of Troyes, Pierre d'Arcis, referred to exhibitions of the Shroud made thirty-four years earlier "or thereabouts." These displays had been investigated at that time by his episcopal predecessor in Troyes, Henri de Poitiers. We might wish that Pierre d'Arcis had been more precise, but his rough date does suggest that showings of the Shroud took place about the time Charny died in 1356 on the battlefield of Poitiers. The bishop stoutly opposed a renewed series of such displays and denounced the motives of those who had made them. But for the purposes of our inquiry the question is whether the earlier showings were made by Charny or by others after his death. Had the pious model knight engaged in practices that later brought episcopal investigation of fraud? The likelihood is that those in charge of Geoffroi's son (the second Geoffroi de Charny, who had inherited the Shroud), caused considerable scandal by their profitable public showings to crowds of pilgrims.

A fascinating piece of evidence appeared with the proper identification only in 1960 of a lead pilgrim's badge, now in a Paris museum. This badge bears an unmistakable representation of the Shroud, the arms of Charny, and those of Geoffroi's second wife, Jeanne de Vergy.[57] It seems at first glance that steps had been taken to encourage a flow of pilgrims to see the Shroud in Charny's lifetime and that this traffic justified the manufacture—and sale—of badges for the faithful to wear in display of their active piety. One of these found its way back to Paris. Yet Victor Saxer makes the plausible suggestion that the arms on the badge could represent not Geoffroi I and his wife but his infant son Geoffroi and his widow. If so, the profitable displays of the Shroud were the work of Jeanne de Vergy and the clerics of the church at Lirey.[58]

Fortunately, we need not get enmeshed in the webs of controversy that have accumulated over the years from scholarly and popular interest in the Shroud. We can note in passing, however, how many of the problems associated with the Shroud would be resolved by the supposition that the cloth was of Eastern manufacture, that Charny obtained it while on crusade in 1345–46, and that he considered it a splendid icon, an aid to pious devotion, rather than an actual relic from the life of Christ.[59] He would not then have felt any need to mention it among the relics of his church at Lirey in his correspondence with the papacy; his possession of the Shroud as icon need not have aroused any controversy at all. Only later, when his widow and the clerics at Lirey blurred the crucial line between icon and relic, did an episcopal investigation lead to charge and countercharge.

Of course these bits of solid evidence and a bit of informed guesswork fail to answer the scores of questions they provoke, but they do suggest that Charny's piety led him to obtain the marvelous cloth he owned. We can recognize that a holy cloth would be a most attractive object of popular devotion at just this time. The cloth known as the Veronica (bearing an imprint of Christ's face), was shown in Rome during the papal jubilee of 1350 and had drawn pilgrims in vast numbers. It is in any case fascinating to realize that in his final years two pieces of sacred cloth, the oriflamme and the Shroud, fittingly represented the major facets of chivalry and religion as they blended in Charny's life.

The Knight and Pious Independence

Through Charny's treatise, then, we can peer into the religious mentality of a respected knight. The view is instructive. His piety appears at first to be as conventional as it is omnipresent. Charny seems almost driven to garnish his text with constant references to Our Lord and the Blessed Virgin. He is at pains to emphasize the need to reverence priests and their sacred services. His prolix piety forms the very framework of his thought as he analyses his own profession of knighthood.

This apparently straightforward, even simplistic piety requires much closer analysis, however. For Charny's piety can easily mask the fundamental layer of lay independence that undergirds it, emerging in places like some geological stratum exposed by weathering. We will not understand Charny if we fail to take into consideration each aspect of his religiosity—his deep piety and a marked spirit of lay independence—or if we fail to recognize the strength of each. Charny's lay piety may seem to be an amalgam fused from seemingly contradictory elements. Yet it can tell us much about the way he made sense of the world around him. If it is personal to its maker, it speaks to much more general issues of chivalry and religion. Knights considered themselves good Christians. They felt a need to fit their violent vocation into the framework of Christian teaching; many if not all of them wanted to understand, as well as buttress, their place of dominance within the increasingly ordered Christian society.

If Charny was the pious owner of the Shroud of Turin, he was also the honored bearer of the Oriflamme, the sacred war banner of the kings of France. Religion of one sort or another was the common thread woven into both emblems, but the combination speaks to a significant degree of lay independence that characterized attitudes of many knights. He was willing to think and act outside the narrow confines prescribed for knighthood by ecclesiastical thinkers. At times he steps around clerical authority with an easy knightly confidence that his beliefs and actions win direct divine approval. Men possessed of sheer physical power in any age tend to use religious ideas to valorize their lives and their social and political control. Some of them have also demonstrated a piety that could spring from deep spirituality. We cannot pretend to know the balance of motive in Charny's mind, let alone the content of his soul. We can only note the evidence that shows when and how Charny parted company with the clerics. He did not unquestioningly accept their high claims to direct and judge the truth of all religious ideas and worth of all practices among the laity.

The touchy issue of sexual morality shows his pragmatic and independent approach. We can contrast it with a clerical view found in the *Queste del Sainte Graal,* one of the romances of the Vulgate or Lancelot-Grail Cycle, written (under Cistercian influence) around 1225. In this book virginity stands at the head of a prominent list of ideal knightly virtues projected into an imagined golden age of chivalry. Early in his adventures Perceval, one of the successful Grail knights, hears how crucially important his virginity is to his high knightly status:

for had your body been violated by the corruption of sin, you would have forfeited your primacy among the Companions of the Quest, even as Lancelot of the Lake, who through the lusts and fevers of the flesh let slip long since the prospects of attaining what all the rest now strive after.[60]

At times in this work the monastic sexual ethic urged on knights takes on an almost hysterical tone. Contrary to such clerically inspired exhortations about virginity, Charny accepts discreet love affairs. There is a sense of balance here. Charny is concerned about encouraging prowess and knows a love can make a warrior more *preux,* that is, more animated by prowess. Thus he looks understandingly aside from a well-conducted love affair. But he is no advocate of casual sex. It will be wise always for the knight, he insists, to think less about the pleasure of his body and more about his soul and his honor. He wants knights to defend their ladies when necessary through their great skill with arms. He does, granted, include in his description of the ceremony of making a knight the placing of a white belt of virginity around his body. This symbol however, is borrowed—as all details of the ceremony seem to be—from a previous work, the *Ordene de chevalerie,* and does not seem central to what he says.[61]. Charny's moderate position between extreme views on sexuality rejects both clerical insistence on virginity and the lay enthusiasts who elevated sexual love to a formal art and a central place in life.

Charny's religious independence may appear most broadly in his sense of the relative status of knighthood in the world. Clerics had developed the idea that human society was composed of divinely ordained professional groups, each called an *ordo.* By the time Charny wrote, the idea of a tripartite division within Christian society occupied a venerable place in medieval thought. The social world was maintained through the respective functions of those who fought, those who prayed, and those who worked. Of course the first two orders, knighthood and priesthood, received the most elaborate theoretical attention. It comes as no surprise to find that clerical writers emphasized the preeminence of their own order. They often invoked the analogy of the soul's superiority to the body. Some lay writers accepted this, but a few romances asserted flatly that chivalry was the highest order God had created.[62]

Charny maneuvers skillfully on this sensitive issue. He is second to none in his formal and conservative reverence for the clergy, especially for the secular clergy (more than the monks) since they perform the mass. But he modulates this hymn of praise so insistently that he ends in a quite different key. In his *Livre Charny* he advises parents how to know which son is to become a knight and which a priest. The son who likes to run, jump, and hit is on the road to knighthood; the son who never wants to sing or laugh should become a priest.[63] In a more serious vein, he gives knights greater praise for their physical suffering and even martyrdom in the *Book of Chivalry*. No cleric earns such merit. After cataloguing the pains and tribulations endured on military campaign, Charny asks pointedly, "And where are the [religious] orders which could suffer as much?" He insists that a good knight can wear his armor as purely and devoutly as any priest wears his vestments for divine service. Moreover, a knight must keep his conduct as thoroughly honest as any priest's, "ou plus (or more)". The necessity to be a good Christian is even more imperative for the knight because he lives in constant peril and must be ready to die at any moment. This point bears weight with Charny, who repeats it more than once: the knight has the greatest need of all to be a good Christian. Since it is harder for the knight, his implication is that he deserves higher merit and status.

One final case of lay independence is instructive. Tournament was the great sport thought essential to chivalric life. It filled many happy days of a knight's life and many pages of the romances he read. Yet clerics had for centuries denounced this mock warfare as unchristian. They had even denied burial in sanctified ground to knights killed in the rough sport. This clerical condemnation had never made much headway against the compelling popularity of joust and tournament in all their particular forms. Kings, too, had tried to control a sport considered dangerous to public order and a convenient cover for mustering anti-royal forces. Yet the checkered pattern of royal prohibitions, royal regulation, and royal sponsorship of tournament had likewise fallen short of really effective control. By the fourteenth century even ecclesiastics seem to have given up with a sigh and a grumble. Kings on both sides of the Channel came to terms with the tournament by becoming its grand sponsor, insofar as they could, especially through the medium of the royal chivalric orders so prominent in Charny's lifetime.[64] The great English knight, Henry, Duke of Lancaster, wrote an acceptance of tournament into his pious treatise written about the same time as Charny's.[65] Even Ramon Llull, the former knight become quasi-friar, had earlier assumed that tournaments occupied honorable space in the life of his model knight.[66] Charny enthusiastically endorsed tournament in all forms. His praise for jousting and fighting in the *mêlée* as the first two honorable levels of prowess does not ruffle the smooth surface of his piety in the slightest. Had he been present generations earlier at the deathbed of the great William Marshal, Charny would surely have nodded in sage agreement with Marshal's classic opinion in response to sharp questioning about his lifetime participation in tournament:

listen to me for a while. The clerks are too hard on us. They shave us too closely. I have captured five hundred knights and have appropriated their arms, horses, and their entire equipment. If for this reason the kingdom of God is closed to me, I can do nothing about it, for I cannot return my booty. I can do no more for God than to give myself to him, repenting all my sins. Unless the clergy desire my damnation, they must ask no more. But their teaching is false—else no one could be saved.[67]

The lay independence so prominent in this declaration stands out in Charny's work. Not only does he accept these "deeds of arms of peace," done in tournament, but even more he lauds the "deeds of arms of war." War, after all, was the supreme theater for the knightly manifestations of prowess that meant so much to him. He thus must progress, however swiftly, through the tangled and prickly field of just war theory in order to reach safe ground on which all the men-at-arms of his audience can use their weapons with clear consciences. He is familiar enough with scholastic doctrine on just war to use the term "necessity" in valorizing knightly warfare. Strictly clerical theory, however, has very little effect in limiting the field of licit warfare in his view. Charny insists on the legitimacy of the fighting in which knights were so constantly engaged in the France of his own day: "for when lords have wars their subjects can and must fight for them." He assures knights that they can enter these battles with moral confidence as well as chivalric gusto. The due and proper service to the lord from whom they hold their lands is best demonstrated by feats of arms. Honorable knights must take the risk of losing it all: life, honor, and possessions. Moreover, with clear conscience they can enter battle to avoid their own disherison or dishonor, or to protect defenseless young women, widows, or orphans. Few conflicts in contemporary Europe could not fit within one of these elastic rubrics. In all such causes, Charny argues, the fighting is beneficial to both body and soul. If they do well with their bodies, the fighting men will win great honor; if they die, their souls are saved—unless, of course, their great sins prevent it.

Charny's treatise, then, allows us to peer into the religious mentality of a respected fourteenth-century knight. His piety forms the very framework of his thought as he analyses his own profession of knighthood, garnishing the text with constant references to Our Lord and his Blessed Mother. Yet he demonstrates a distinct knightly independence whenever issues essential to chivalry might generate clerical critiques. He is certain there can be no contradiction between a worthy knightly vocation and true religion.

This point is worth emphasizing for piety and chivalry do not occupy separate spaces in his consciousness. For Charny, piety and chivalry form inseparable, almost interchangeable qualities in men of war. Through the hard martyrdom of their profession knights acted in accordance with God's will and won his approval. So clear was this certainty in Charny's mind that clerical cavils about this particular point or that could be shrugged off as nonessential. The order of chivalry was the keystone that kept the great arch of Charny's world standing firm. What other order could compare with it? The essential role of the clergy in a sacramental religion was obvious to him. Yet Charny believed that in broad domains of their lives the great host of his warriors served God without a need to acknowledge the stringencies of ecclesiastical control. Right order in the world (including, of course, true religion) was secured finally through the power and self-sacrificing service of the Order of Knighthood. This was the essence of knightly lay piety, not its qualification or denial. Spiritual rectitude and physical force fused in the knightly mission. As Maurice Keen has acutely observed, Charny ends his book appropriately with a combination prayer and war cry: "Pray to God for him who is the author of this book he has now finished. Charni, Charny."[68]

Forming the Perfect Worthy Man

In Charny's mind all of the desirable qualities of prowess and piety come together to perfection in what he calls the worthy man (*preudomme*). Time and again he assures his audience that the motives of all good men-at-arms can always be read as honorable. But again, as with prowess, he proposes a scale. A true man of worth, will have moved through several stages in each of three essential categories of worthiness. Only one who has achieved the best in all three categories ranks as a worthy man.

First, he will have progressed beyond simple-minded goodness and the formalities of charity and church attendance to genuine love and service of God. Second, his intelligence will not be of the merely malicious or merely subtle sort, but will have attained what is good and reasonable. Third, he will show valor beyond the disorderly type found in seekers of individual good only; he will demonstrate a more mature prowess in military action abroad as well as at home, following good leaders. He will even have become a seasoned commander himself, wise in his military experience. The man who combines in his own actions the final stage of each category Charny says will be the ideal layman, "supreme among all lay people," the model for emulation.

Can such a combination of qualities be found in a single man? Charny is pragmatic. He expects knights to aspire to greatness, but he never demands that they achieve perfection. A fascinating list of historical examples makes just this point. Even the greatest men from biblical and classical times revealed flaws. Charny's highly personal choices include Samson, Absalom, St. Peter, and Julius Caesar. All failed in at least one aspect of what he considers their good chivalry. Yet he also wants a single great example to remind men to aspire for perfection. He cites that "holy knight" Judas Maccabeus from the Hebrew scriptures. This hero of Ancient Israel, Charny assures his audience, was indeed the ideal knight, motivated by piety and prowess, endowed, guided and rewarded by God (Section 35). Above all, Charny reminds his contemporaries, such perfection can never be attributed to human effort alone, but rather to God's wonderful grace. Like the Calvinists of later centuries, Charny powerfully combines the most urgent calls for strenuous human effort with the most thorough sense of absolute divine election.

There can be no thought that a life of fighting counts against a man-at-arms in the eyes of God. Though some say a man cannot save his soul through fighting, Charny assures his audience that men can save or lose their souls in any profession. But Charny is, of course, interested in knights, not bakers or merchants, and one suspects that he thinks God is inclined in the same martial direction. The knight's arms, Charny insists, are those of God when he uses them to secure reason and right, when he calls for divine help. Those who fight well but die in the fray need not fear; they will be taken into God's select company to enjoy paradise forever. His terms are never so explicit, but perhaps in his musings he pictured an otherworldly Company of Heaven replacing and perfecting the earthly Company of the Star.

In all such lines of thought, Charny shows a very important general trend in the way in which knights came to think of their hard lives and good service. They eagerly absorbed the fulsome praise clerics had for centuries lavished on knighthood. In large measure, however, they managed to ignore the highly discriminating nature of this praise. In effect they filtered out all the implicit critiques and all the careful advice intended to guide and control knightly behavior. Clerics intended to praise only the subset of knights who were willing to reform their lives according to one clerical plan or another. Knights seem to have generalized such praise to all of knighthood. At most they might exclude a very small set of admittedly rotten fellows.

Charny shows the tendency clearly. In effect he turns St Bernard on his head by thinking of the majority of knights as splendid fellows and only a small minority as utter failures. The proportions of the elect and the reprobate in St Bernard's view have been reversed; most knights now merit the praise St. Bernard lavished on the select few. Only a minority of fourteenth-century knights, Charny professes to believe, merit the vitriolic criticisms the great Cistercian had poured on knighthood in general. Of course St. Bernard and Charny both believed in hard service and even martyrdom in a good cause. This meant winning the approval of God who sacrificed himself for his people. Charny and St Bernard also share disapproval of the foolishness of vain display, rather than true and disciplined service. Yet the wrongs that most concern Charny are clearly quite different from those that troubled St Bernard. The political and military realities in France by the middle of the fourteenth century left him little choice. He is desperately worried that prowess had atrophied. Good knights must show good prowess.

The subject of the bad knight leaves a bitter taste in Charny's mouth and he touches on it only briefly, expressly stating his great relief when he can return to talk of the good knights. Even when he dispenses seemingly casual advice, especially to young aspirants for knighthood, Charny warns against some enemy of prowess—living to eat, sleeping late in soft beds, and so forth. Timidity, even more than sloth or indolence, is the insidious enemy of prowess. When he writes of the cowardly warrior Charny comes as close to humor as his dignity and a high sense of mission will allow. His humor, however, is dark and biting. How else could he deal with men of war who have failed to understand the great lesson that it is better to die with honor intact than to live shamefully? In these passages he writes a more withering sarcasm than any contemporary chronicler. Always the reformer, though, he carefully defines the focus of his target. Not all French knights are to blame. Certainly the chivalry he advocates—if only the will to exercise it can be restored—will produce prowess that matches the enemy blow for blow, come what may. The good knight will not retreat from a battle, but will stand his ground and do all the harm he can to his enemies.

If unworthy knights lacked prowess, they also fell short of that second great chivalric virtue, loyalty. Only loyalty can assure the necessary hierarchy and stalwart fighting that is justifiable and ennobling. Factionalism among the French nobility had generated a good deal of in-fighting. Even Charny's generous standards could not classify most of this conflict as legitimate. Some men, he admits, wear armor but are not really good men-at-arms. These dishonest, disorderly men make war without reason and seize, rob and wound people without the proper defiance. Others may avoid such direct misdeeds, but act in this fashion through their subordinates and receive them after the fact. Such men, he sternly warns, are unworthy to live or to enjoy the company of truly good men-at-arms. The pains and hardships these men incur in fighting are not signs of their virtue, but a foretaste of the greater pains that await them in hell.

In the meantime, had the Company of the Star developed along the lines its founder intended, any members of the Company inclined to do dishonorable deeds were threatened with a foretaste of hell. The rules of the Company mandated periodic public recounting of all knightly adventures, honorable or otherwise, in a full meeting of the knightly order. Public shame awaited the bad knights. Moreover, all deeds—again, the vile no less than the valorous—would be immortalized in the book kept by three clerks. The idea seems to have been borrowed from the Arthurian court as pictured in literature of the age. The Company of the Star, guided by Charny's treatise, could provide both the carrot and the stick to urge knights toward honor in this life and its reward in the next. Let all aspire to be worthy men!

As modern readers we will likely be inclined to interpret the great chivalric virtue of loyalty in national or at least in royal terms. Loyalty to the crown and to the French state, it will seem, must surely constitute the core of this virtue. We need to be cautious. In some dimensions kings and knights shared goals; in other dimensions their interests clashed. Charny was loyal to his king and grateful for the many favors and honors his sovereign had bestowed. Likewise, he clearly worried over the humiliating invasions of the kingdom of France. Yet we need to see that to a great French knight loyalty meant adherence to chivalry as much as anything else. A loyal man was steady and predictable in following the chivalric ideal, not false and changeable.

To attract loyalty kings had to show great virtues and a great sense of duty. In two lengthy lists of rhetorical questions, filling half a dozen folio pages of the text (Section 24), Charny elaborates the reasons why kings and princes exist. The first list suggests the possibility of a thoroughly disreputable conception of kingship. Should rulers see authority simply as license for ease, private enrichment at common expense, and cowardice and neglect of defense? Charny answers each of these questions with a resounding negative: kingship cannot have such origins. The second set of questions asks whether true kingship is based on good governance in war and peace. Charny gives an enthusiastically positive answer to each question. His views here are conventional but powerfully expressed. In his effort to make the point clear he makes it repeatedly: kings have been chosen because they have the strength to suffer the pains needed to work for good governance. The basis of authority is a sense of duty, not entitlement to ease and empty mastery. By stating his case in two long catalogues of rhetorical questions, turning each negative statement into a positive injunction for good governance, Charny doubles the impact of his message. He likewise balances his mini-sermon on current problems with a defense of the proper functioning of kingship.

Yet we must remember our caution. Kingship and chivalry were not always compatible. Charny and Jean le Bon cooperated in a time of crisis that demanded unity if the accustomed social and political order of the kingdom were to survive. Earlier kings and knights often saw their relationship in different terms; they were acting in different circumstances, and were less committed to the necessity of reform measures. Kings were themselves knights, but knew they had responsibilities and God-given powers beyond any knight. Many knights clearly thought of themselves as kinglets. They could manage very well in deciding issues of justice and war without the governance of kings.

The legitimate use of force was a particular sticking point. Many French lords had long claimed the use of force as their legitimate right.

They expected to be able to fight licitly what are often called private wars. In fact, they would have claimed this right for each of the many causes in Charny's generous list in the *Book of Chivalry*. But their claims were coming to be contested by the growing reality of royal sovereignty. For the king claimed superior rights where violence was concerned. The king wanted at least a supervisory right over its use. Vigorous monarchs had brought into their courts whole classes of actions in which one side had proceeded "by force and arms, against the king's peace," or "by illegal and prohibited arms."[69] Such phrases contrast sharply with Charny's statement of approval for honor achieved "by force of arms and through good deeds." As Philippe Contamine has observed of Charny, "In his eyes, the war of the king of France is in no way privileged; it appears as only one of the guises which the profession of arms could wear."[70]

In Charny's own lifetime the crown was busy regulating private war between knights within the realm.[71] A royal act of 1338–39 confirmed for Aquitaine the right of lords in that duchy to war against each other, but insisted they respect certain conditions. The two sides must respectively give and accept formal notification of the war and they must likewise cease their war at the commencement of the king's own war. An act of 1352 renewed the prohibition of private wars during royal war, and another edict in 1354 affirmed the concept of the Quarantaine le Roy (attributed to Saint Louis), which imposed a forty-day truce during which relatives of the principals involved could declare their intentions regarding the war.

It would be fascinating to know Charny's reaction to such royal measures. If he is a royalist, he is also much in favor of the very chivalric practice of war within the realm which French kings were trying to bring within the sphere of their control. Problems between kings and knights stemmed from overlapping claims in just such cases. The tension is inherent; it did not emerge simply from knights who regrettably could not live up to the high standards of chivalry. Knightly great deeds could cut against the grain of royal claims.

Yet Charny's book does not always treat of the mountain peaks of great deeds or great issues. He is, as we have seen, a pragmatic writer. At times—especially in the section of "Advice for the Young Knight" (Section 19)—the spirit of his book seems almost appropriate to the modern athletic field, with Charny playing the familiar role of coach. We find him giving the lads advice that will serve them for the game of life as well as the martial game at hand. As you enter the fray, he says, never think of what your opponent can do to you; think rather of what you are going to

do to him. Praise others, do not boast of yourself. Guard your own honor
"sovereignly," but never let envy keep you from honoring others. Never
quarrel with a fool or a drunk. Steer clear of prostitutes. Love the ladies,
but never boast of your conquests. Avoid sleeping late in soft beds and
eating too much fine food. Time is too important to waste. Sometimes
the lesser side in a struggle wins; this happens in the world, but it cannot
last, for it is contrary to reason. He is realistic. While he warns sternly
against the vice of gambling, for example, he knows his audience and
knows that they will be "determined to play" with dice. His admonition
therefore shifts to a warning against excess and especially about the risk of
anger. Perhaps the parent as well as the coach appears when he exclaims
that all who survive youth honestly must praise God all their lives for it.

Was the text he wrote really important in the history of chivalry? Was
it widely read and influential? It seems highly unlikely that Charny's text
ever found a wide readership, certainly nothing at all comparable to the
audience intended. It was planned to radiate a set of ideas through the
Company of the Star into French chivalric society and perhaps to knights
in general. The utter collapse of the Company of the Star sank any hope
for the influence of Charny's *Book of Chivalry*. But the importance of
Geoffroi and his book rest finally with us rather than with a diminishing
audience of knightly readers in fourteenth- or fifteenth-century Europe.
As students of his age we can profitably listen to his ideas with greater
attentiveness than did his contemporaries. He has much to teach us about
a demanding code of behavior, about a thought-provoking combination
of piety with violence. We have yet to find satisfying answers to the unset-
tling questions his book and his life raise—about masculine violence, a
code of honor, and their relationship to religion.

A Note on the Manuscripts Used

The English translation of *Le livre de chevalerie* is based on two French
manuscripts: Brussels, Bibliothèque Royale de Belgique: 1124–26, ff 83–
136; and Paris, Bibliothèque Nationale, nouvelle acquisitions française,
4736, ff 36–87. The former text was used as the base manuscript for the
translation. The latter manuscript breaks off before the end of the text and
is more troubled by omissions. Elspeth Kennedy provides a full discussion
of the manuscripts and the editorial procedures she followed in setting
the text and making her translation in Richard W. Kaeuper and Elspeth

Kennedy, *The Book of Chivalry of Geoffroi de Charny* (Philadelphia, University of Pennyslvania Press, 1996), 67–81.

Notes

1. The classic book is Maurice Keen, *Chivalry* (New Haven, Conn., 1984). Cf Richard W. Kaeuper, *Chivalry and Violence in Medieval Europe* (Oxford, 1999).

2. R. W. Southern, *Western Society and the Church in the Middle Ages* (Harmondsworth, 1970), 39.

3. Keen, *Chivalry*, 18–43.

4. *Polycraticus*, ed. C. C. J. Webb, CVII, ch. 21 (Oxford, 1909).

5. William Caxton printed an English version, *The Book of the Ordre of Chyvalry*, ed. Alfred T. P. Byles, EETS (London, 1926).

6. Two other texts join Charny's, in a trinity of works very close to knighthood, the *History of William Marshal*, vol. 1, *Text and Translation*, ed. A. J. Holden, trans. S. Gregory and David Crouch, Anglo-Norman Text Society (London, 2002) and Sir Thomas Malory's *Morte Darthur*, in Thomas Malory, *Works*, ed. Eugene Vinaver (Oxford, 1971).

7. For overviews of his life, see Keen, *Chivalry*, 12; Philippe Contamine, "Geoffroy de Charny (début du XIVe siècle–1356), 'Le plus prudhomme et le plus vaillant de tous les autres,'"in *Histoire et société: mélanges Georges Duby*, 4 vols., vol. 2, *Le tenancier, le fidèle et le citoyen* (Aix-en-Provence, 1992), 107–21. Cf. Jean Froissart, *Chroniques de Jean Froissart*, ed. Siméon Luce (Paris, 1869–99), IV, xxxi, n. 2, citing Archives Nationales JJ 84, 671.

8. Classic older histories of the war include Édouard Perroy, *The Hundred Years War* (New York, 1965) and Jean Favier, *La Guerre de cent ans* (Paris, 1980). For more recent accounts see Jonathon Sumption, *The Hundred Years War*, two vols. (Philadelphia, 1992, 1999); Anne Curry, *The Hundred Years War* (Houndmills, Basingstoke, 1993); Clifford J. Rodgers, *The Wars of Edward III: Sources and Interpretation* (Woodbridge, 1999).

9. Raymond Cazelles, *Société politique, noblesse et couronne sous Jean le Bon et Charles V* (Paris, 1982), 13.

10. A brief description of the battle and a full set of sources appear in Sumption, *The Hundred Years War*, vol. 1, *Trial by Battle*, 402. That Talbot was Charny's battlefield captor appears in Adam Murimuth's chronicle: *Adae Murimuth, continuatio Chronicarum Robertus de Avesbury, De Gestis Mirabilibus Regis Edwardi Tertii*, ed. Edward M. Thompson, Rolls Series 93 (London, 1889), 129.

11. *Calendar of Patent Rolls, 1343–45*, 130.

12. Arthur Piaget, "Le Livre Messire Geoffroi de Charny," *Romania* 26 (1897), 394. Jonathan Riley-Smith provides an overview and excellent maps in *The Atlas of the Crusades* (New York, 1991), 140–41. Details regarding this crusade come from Aziz S. Atiya, "The Crusade in the Fourteenth Century," 12; Deno Geanakoplos, "Byzantium and the Crusades, 1354–1453," 61–62; Peter Topping, "The Morea, 1311–1364," 133, all in *A History of the Crusades*, gen. ed. Kenneth M.

Setton, 4 vols., vol. 3., *The Fourteenth and Fifteenth Centuries*, ed. Harry W. Hazard (Madison, Wis., 1969–89).

13. Steven Runciman, *A History of the Crusades*, vol. 3, *The Kingdom of Acre and the Later Crusades* (Cambridge, 1951–54), 452.

14. Cazelles, *Société politique*, 121–26; Favier, *La Guerre de cent ans*, 127; Perroy, *Hundred Years War*, 121; John Bell Henneman, *Royal Taxation in Medieval France: The Development of War Financing (1322–1356)* (Princeton, N.J., 1971), 227–38.

15. *Oeuvres complètes de Froissart*, ed. Kervyn de Lettenhove (Brussels, 1867–77), V, 229–30.

16. The account that follows draws on Froissart's several accounts and on the information in Contamine, "Geoffroy de Charny," 112.

17. Chandos Herald, *Life of the Black Prince by the Herald of Sir John Chandos*, ed. Mildred K. Pope and Eleanor C. Lodge (Oxford, 1910), ll. 415–75.

18. *Issues of the Exchequer*, ed. Frederick Devon (London, 1837), 156, 157.

19. *Oeuvres de Froissart*, ed. Lettenhove, V, 246–47.

20. Ibid, 250.

21. Ibid., XX, 544.

22. According to Lettenhove the ransom was 1000 écus. *Oeuvres de Froissart*, XX, 543. Père Anselme states that it was 12,000 écus. Père F. Anselme, *Histoire généalogique et chronologique de la Maison royale de France, des pairs, grands officiers de la Couronne et de la Maison du roy et des anciens barons du royaume* (Paris, 1967), 201.

23. *Chronique normande du XIVe siècle*, ed. Auguste Molinier and Emile Molinier (Paris, 1882), 101.

24. *Oeuvres de Froissart*, V, 271–74. Cf. *Chronique normande du XIVe siècle*, ed. Molinier and Molinier, 103–4 and *Chronique des quatre premiers Valois*, ed. Siméon Luce (Paris, 1862), 29–30.

25. *Oeuvres de Froissart*, XVII, 293–94.

26. What follows is based on D'Arcy Jonathan Dacre Boulton, *Knights of the Crown: The Monarchical Orders of Knighthood in Later Medieval Europe, 1325–1520* (New York, 1987), 167–210.

27. Ibid., 186.

28. For what follows see Philippe Contamine, "L'Oriflamme de Saint-Denis aux XIVe et XVe siècles," *Annales de l'Est* 7 (1973), 179–244. Anselme gives the 1355 date, but cites other sources that indicate 1347. Anselme, *Histoire généalogique*, 202.

29. R. Delachanel, *Histoire de Charles V* (Paris, 1909), 226, citing sources. In his *Life of the Black Prince*, 55, the Chandos Herald quotes Charny's speech.

30. Combining into one narrative Froissart's slightly differing accounts: *Oeuvres de Froissart*, V, 443, 453.

31. Lettenhove mentions Charny's rescue of the king in *Oeuvres de Froissart*, V, 543. Alfred Coville likewise mentions this incident, *Les premiers Valois et la Guerre de cent ans (1328–1422)*, vol. 4 of *Histoire de France depuis les origines jusqu'à la Révolution*, ed. Ernest Lavisse (Paris, 1901–1910, reprint New York, 1969),

107. Froissart's description of the capture of Jean II appears in *Oeuvres de Froissart*, V, 433–34, 453–54.

32. Contamine, "Geoffroy de Charny," 114; *Oeuvres de Froissart*, XX, 525, 543; Anselme, *Histoire généalogique*, 201; Jean Rossbach, ed., "Les demandes pour la joute, le tournoi, et la guerre de Geoffroy de Charny (XIVème siècle)," Ph.D. dissertation, University of Brussels, 1961," 137; Cazelles, *Société politique*, 527–28.

33. *Oeuvres de Froissart*, V, 412: "Le plus preudomme et le plus vailant de tous les autres."

34. Geoffrey le Baker, *Chronicon Galfridi le Baker de Swynebroke*, ed. Edward M. Thompson (Oxford, 1889), 103.

35. Steven Muhlberger edits, translates, and comments on these questions in Geoffroi de Charny, *Jousts and Tournaments: Charny and the Rules for Chivalric Sport in Fourteenth-Century France*, trans. Steven Muhlberger (Union City, Calif., 2002). They are also printed in French in Michael Anthony Taylor, ed., "A Critical Edition of Geoffroy de Charny's 'Livre Charny' and the 'Demandes pour la joute, le tournois et la guerre,'" Ph.D. dissertation, University of North Carolina at Chapel Hill, 1977, 24–34.

36. Muhlberger, *Jousts and Tournaments*; cf Taylor, ed., "Critical Edition," 24–34.

37. Jean LeClercq notes how much the knightly life is for Bernard a matter of asceticism and discipline. "Saint Bernard's Attitude Toward War," in *Studies in Medieval Cistercian History, II*, ed. John R. Sommerfeldt (Kalamazoo, Mich., 1976).

38. Bernard de Clairvaux, *On Grace and Free Choice: Praise of the New Knighthood*, in *The Works of Bernard of Clairvaux*, vol. 7, *Treatises III*, trans. Daniel O'Donovan and Conrad Greenia, Cistercian Father Series 19 (Kalamazoo, Mich., 1977), 127–67.

39. See Norris J. Lacy, gen. ed, *Lancelot-Grail: The Old French Arthurian Vulgate and Post-Vulgate in Translation*, 5 vols. (New York, 1993–96).

40. Jean Fillon de Venette, *The Chronicle of Jean de Venette*, trans. Jean Birdsall, ed. Richard A. Newhall (New York, 1953), 45.

41. Ibid., 62–63.

42. The *Grandes Chroniques de France*, ed. Jules Viard, Société de l'Histoire de France 9 (Paris, 1937), in sections written between 1344 and 1350.

43. The continuator of the Chronicle of Guilliaume de Nangis, quoted in Charles de Beaurepaire, "Complainte sur la bataille de Poitiers," *Bibliothèque de l'Ecole des Chartes* 12, ser. III, 2 (1850), 259.

44. Discussed and printed by André Vernet, "Le tragicum argumentum de miserabili statu regni Francie de François de Monte Belluna (1357)," *Annuaire-Bulletin de la Société de l'Histoire de France* (1962–63).

45. Boulton, *Knights of the Crown*, 196.

46. Noël Denholm-Young, "The Tournament in the Thirteenth Century," in *Studies in Medieval History Presented to Frederick Maurice Powicke*, ed. R. W. Hunt, W. H. Pantin, and R. W. Southern (Oxford, 1948), 260, and Malcolm Vale, *War and Chivalry: Warfare and Aristocratic Culture in England, France, and*

Burgundy at the End of the Middle Ages (Norwich, 1981), 67; note the general use of these categories.

47. A theme of Kaeuper, *Chivalry and Violence.*

48. Quoted in *Chroniques de Jean Froissart*, I, 2.

49. John Gillingham, "Richard I and the Science of War in the Middle Ages," in *War and Government in the Middle Ages: Essays in Honour of J. O. Prestwich*, ed. John Gillingham and J. C. Holt (Bury St. Edmunds, 1984), 78–92; John Gillingham, "War and Chivalry in the *History of William the Marshal*," in *Proceedings of the Newcastle Upon Tyne Conference, 1987*, ed. P. R. Coss and S. D. Lloyd, Thirteenth-Century England 2 (Bury St. Edmunds, 1988), 1–15.

50. Gillingham, "War and Chivalry," 6.

51. Clifford J. Rogers, "The Age of the Hundred Years War," in *Medieval Warfare: A History*, ed. Maurice Keen (Oxford, 1999), 136–37.

52. *Livre Charny*, ll. 363B593, in Taylor, ed., "Critical Edition," quotation at 457–58. For other references to martyrdom, see ll. 130ff, 863.

53. For what follows, see Pietro Savio, "Ricerche sopra la Santa Sindone," *Pontificium Athenaeum Salesianum* 1 (1955), 120–55, which prints the documents, 112. André Perrett, "Essai sur l'histoire du Saint Suaire du XIVe au XVIe siècle," *Académie des Sciences, Belles-lettres, et Arts de Savoie, Mémoires* ser. 6 , IV (1960), 61, argues that Anselme, the source for the amortisement of 1343, must have misread the date, which should be corrected to a decade later. Savio prints Anselme's statement and the papal document (with the 1343 date) in "Ricerche sopra la Santa Sindone," 122.

54. For the results of controlled testing carried out by mass spectrometry (first developed at the University of Rochester) in laboratories in Arizona, Oxford, and Zurich, see P. E. Damon et al., "Radiocarbon Dating of the Shroud of Turin," *Nature* 337 (1989), 611–15, and two articles by Harry E. Gove, "Progress in Radiocarbon Dating the Shroud of Turin," *Radiocarbon* 31 (1989), 965–69, and "Dating the Turin Shroud—An Assessment," *Radiocarbon* 32 (1990), 87–92.

55. Alan D. Adler, "Updating Recent Studies on the Shroud of Turin," in *Archaeological Chemistry: Organic, Inorganic, and Biochemical Analysis*, ed. Mary Virginia Orna, American Chemical Society Symposium Series 625 (Washington, D.C., 1996), 223–39.

56. A clear discussion and many sources appear in Harry E. Gove, *From Hiroshima to the Iceman: The Development and Application of Accelerator Mass Spectrometry* (Philadelphia, 1999). Once again, I am grateful to Professor Gove for useful discussions of the scientific evidence. Peter Schirtzinger and Benjamin Tejblum provided valuable research assistance on scholarship about dating the Shroud.

57. Arthur Forgeais, *Collection de plombs historiés trouvés dans la Seine* (Paris, 1865), 105–8 described and published a drawing of this badge, but he incorrectly identified it as the Shroud of Besançon. The correction appears in Perrett, "Essai sur l'histoire du Saint Suaire," 62. A photograph of the badge appears among the illustrations between pages 226 and 227 in Ian Wilson, *The Shroud of Turin* (New York, 1978). The badge is at present in the Musée de Cluny, Paris (Ref. 75 CN 5261).

58. Victor Saxer, "Le Suaire de Turin aux prises avec l'histoire," *Revue d'Histoire de l'Eglise de France* 76 (1990), 21–55.

59. See the interesting article of W. S. A. Dale, "The Shroud of Turin: Relic or Icon?" *Nuclear Instruments and Methods in Physics Research* 29 (1987), 187–92.

60. *The Quest of the Holy Grail,* trans. Pauline M. Matarasso (Harmondsworth, 1969), 102. See *La Queste del Saint Graal, roman du XIII siècle,* ed. Albert Pauphilet (Paris, 1923), 80, for the original French. Statements showing the radical emphasis on virginity appear throughout the sections of this romance devoted to Lancelot and Perceval.

61. Edited by Keith Busby in *Le Roman des Eles . . . and the Anonymous Ordene de chevalerie,* Utrecht Publications in General and Comparative Literature 17 (Amsterdam, 1983).

62. Chrétien de Troyes, *Le roman de Perceval ou le conte du graal,* ed. William Roach (Geneva, 1956), ll. 1632–35: "Le plus haute ordene . . . Que Diex ait faite et comandee: C'est l'ordre de chevalerie."

63. *Livre Charny,* ll. 1390–1440, in Taylor, ed., "Critical Edition."

64. Kaeuper, *War, Justice and Public Order: England and France in the Later Middle Ages* (Oxford, 1988), 199–211; Boulton, *Knights of the Crown,* passim.

65. *Le Livre de seyntz medicines: The Unpublished Devotional Treatise of Henry of Lancaster,* ed. E. J. Arnould, Anglo-Norman Text Society (Oxford, 1940), 78. Lancaster was one of the original knights of the Garter.

66. *Book of the Ordre of Chyvalry,* ed. Byles, 31, 75.

67. Quoted from Sidney Painter, *William Marshal, Knight-Errant, Baron, and Regent of England* (Baltimore, 1933), 285–86.

68. Maurice H. Keen, "Chivalry, Nobility, and the Man at Arms," in *War, Literature, and Politics in the Late Middle Ages,* ed. C. T. Allmand (Liverpool, 1976).

69. Kaeuper, *War, Justice and Public Order,* 244, 264.

70. Contamine, *Guerre, état et société,* 187. He returns to this theme in "Geoffroy de Charny," 115.

71. For the royal measures that follow, see *Ordonnances des rois de France,* ed. E.-J Laurière et al., 22 vols. (Paris, 1723–1849), vol. 2, 61–63, 552–53.

The Book of Chivalry

Introduction

1 Because I am minded to examine the various conditions of men-at-arms, both of the past and of the present, I want to give some brief account of them. And it is right to do so for all such matters are honorable, although some are honorable enough, others more honorable on an ascending scale up to the most honorable of all. And always the noblest way rises above all others, and those who have the greatest heart for it go constantly forward to reach and achieve the highest honor, and for this reason we must start by speaking of these matters from the beginning. 5

2 First, let us turn to the lesser before moving to the greater; and it seems to me that no one should be dissatisfied by this method of proceeding, for no one will be able to say that in what is written there is anything other than the good and the true; otherwise it would not be right to tell of it. I therefore want to speak of divers conditions of men-at-arms in the best way that I can, for it is right that each of us should record what is good, where there is nothing bad, in relation to all men-at-arms who willingly take up arms for whatsoever form of the practice of them. Where there is no reproach, there can be no evil but only good. For this reason I pray that God may grant me that I do justice to my subject as far as both manner and matter are concerned. 5 ... 10

The Scale of Prowess and Types of Men-at-Arms

3 We shall first speak of a class of men-at-arms who are worthy of praise in terms of the kind of pursuit of arms they are willing to undertake. These are the ones who are physically strong and skillful (agile) and who conduct themselves properly and pleasantly, as is appropriate for young men, gentle, courteous and well mannered toward others, who have no desire to engage in any evil undertaking, but are so eager to perform deeds of arms at jousts that if they hear of any festivities or other occasions for jousting, they will be there if they can; if all goes well for them they will usually win their contest or be in the running for the prize. And because God has bestowed 5

on them such grace as to conduct themselves well in this particular pursuit   10
of arms, they enjoy it so much that they neglect and abandon the other
pursuits of arms; that is not to deny that it is a good pursuit, attractive for
the participants and fair to see. I therefore say that it is good to do for him
who does it, when, by the grace of God he does it well; for all deeds of arms
merit praise for all those who perform well in them. For I maintain that   15
there are no small feats of arms, but only good and great ones, although
some feats of arms are of greater worth than others. Therefore, I say that
he who does more is of greater worth.

Deeds of Arms at Tournaments

4   We should then talk of another pursuit at which many men-at-arms
aim to make their reputation: that is at deeds of arms at tournaments. And
indeed, they earn men praise and esteem for they require a great deal
of wealth, equipment and expenditure, physical hardship, crushing and
wounding, and sometimes danger of death. For this kind of practice of   5
arms, there are some whose physical strength, skill, and agility enable them
to perform so well that they achieve in this activity such great renown for
their fine exploits; and because they often engage in it, their renown and
their fame increases in their own territory and that of their neighbors; thus
they want to continue this kind of pursuit of arms because of the success   10
God has granted them in it. They content themselves with this particular
practice of arms because of the acclaim they have already won and still expect to win from it. Indeed they are worthy of praise; nevertheless he who
does more is of greater worth.

Deeds of Arms in Local Wars

5   After speaking of the above-mentioned peacetime activities in the practice of arms, I should now turn to another category of men-at-arms, those
involved in war, for many aim to make their reputations in this calling in a
number of different ways. I shall therefore speak first of those who seek out
and participate in the wars in their own locality without going into distant
regions and who deserve praise for their great exploits and undertakings
which they have achieved and are achieving by their good sense, their physical strength and dexterity as those who have to wage war on their own
behalf in order to defend their honor and inheritance, or those who want
to wage war to assist in the defense of the honor and inheritance of their
kinsmen, or like those who stay to serve in the wars to defend the honor
and inheritance of their rightful lord who maintains them, for the faith and
loyalty which they owe to their lord cannot be better demonstrated than by
serving him and assisting him loyally in such urgent need as that of war
which is so grave as to put person, land and resources all at risk.

Deeds of Arms in Local Wars

6   There are others still who want to serve their friends or kinsmen, when
they are at war, and there are some who have not the means to leave their
own locality. And when God by his grace grants that such people as are
mentioned above perform great exploits, fight well and distinguish themselves in several successful days of combat which they may have, such people
should be valued and honored who have conducted themselves so well
within their own region. It seems indeed that they would also have done
well elsewhere. And I am prepared to say that all men-at-arms who have
done well in this art of war and who have often been successful, even if it
were only in their own district, should be honored among all men in their
own locality as one should honor good men-at-arms and as is appropriate
in relation to such a very noble activity as the practice of arms in war, which
surpasses all other except the service of God.

Deeds of Arms in War Are the Most Honorable

7   We have spoken of those men, and of the men-at-arms who in their own
region, perform deeds of arms in the way which seems best to them; indeed
no one should speak except in favorable and honorable terms, especially in
relation to armed exploits in war, in whatever region, provided that they
are performed without reproach. But it seems to me that in the practice of
arms in war it is possible to perform in one day all the three different kinds

of military art, that is jousting, tourneying, and waging war, for war requires jousting with the point of the lance and striking with the edge of the
sword as in a tournament, and attacking with the swordthrust and other
weapons, as war demands. Therefore one should value and honor men-at-   10
arms engaged in war more highly than any other men-at-arms; for in the
practice or arms in jousts some are pleased enough with what they do without undertaking any other deeds of arms. The same is true in relation to
tournaments, for some are satisfied with taking part just in them and not in
any other use of arms. And these two uses of arms are both to be found in   15
armed combat in war. It is therefore a great and honorable thing that these
uses of arms, of which some feel they have achieved enough by performing
just one, should all be carried out together by men-at-arms engaged in war
each day they have to fight on the battlefield. For this reason you should
love, value, praise, and honor all those whom God by his grace has granted   20
several good days on the battlefield, when they win great credit and renown
for their exploits; for it is from good battles that great honors arise and are
increased, for good fighting men prove themselves in good battles, where
they show their worth in their own locality without traveling outside it. We
have now dealt with those good men-at-arms who have fought well in their   25
own region and have found good battles to take part in.

8   We shall next consider another category of men-at-arms, those who in-
tend to make their reputation, traveling outside their own territory, in several different ways, which are all good and honorable, although some are of
greater value than others.

Men-at-Arms Who Undertake Distant Journeys and Pilgrimages
9   We shall first consider those who aim to make their reputation by a
great enterprise, undertaking distant journeys and pilgrimages in several
far-away and foreign countries; they may thereby see many strange and
unusual things at which other men who have not traveled abroad would
wonder because of the strange marvels and extraordinary things described   5
by those men who have seen them; and those who listen can scarcely believe
what they hear, and some say mockingly that it is all lies. And it should
seem to all men of worth that those who have seen such things can and
should give a better and truer account of them than those who will not or
dare not go there, nor should nor can any one reasonably say, without hav-   10
ing been there, that such people lie. We should therefore be glad to listen
to, behold, and honor those who have been on distant journeys to foreign

parts, for indeed no one can travel so far without being many times in physical danger. We should for this reason honor such men-at-arms who at great expense, hardship, and grave peril undertake to travel to and see dis- 15 tant countries and strange things, although, to tell the truth, among all those who are intent on distant journeys, there are some who make a habit of it and who always want to go and see new and strange things and do not stay anywhere long and cannot find and take part in armed exploits as often as others who do not seek out such very distant journeys and who stay 20 longer in one place and wait for the opportunity to perform great deeds of arms in war. It may well happen that in making these distant journeys they may from time to time encounter some fine adventure, but not very often, for when, in the midst of a time of peace, it is possible to go where one would not dare to go equipped for war nor as a man-at-arms, but only as a 25 pilgrim or a merchant. It seems therefore to some that one does not come across opportunities to practice the military art so often in this way of life as might be encountered in another way of life. Nevertheless one should honor and respect such men who subject themselves in this way to physical danger and hardship in order to see these strange things and make distant 30 journeys. And they find satisfaction in doing this because of the won-drously strange things which they have seen and still want to see. And in-deed it is a fine thing, but nevertheless I say: he who does more is of greater worth.

Deeds Performed Outside One's Locality for Pay or Other Rewards

10   Now we must consider yet another category of men-at-arms who deserve much praise. That is those who, for various compelling reasons which need not be mentioned here, leave their locality, perhaps for the profit they might expect to get from this, which might be greater than any-thing they could obtain in their own locality. And in this way they leave 5 their locality before they have gained any reputation there, and they would have preferred to remain in their own region if they could well do so. But nevertheless they leave and go to Lombardy or Tuscany or Pulia or other lands where pay or other rewards can be earned, and there they stay and are provided with horses, and armor is included in the pay and rewards they 10 receive. Through this they can see, learn and gain knowledge of much that is good through participating in war, for they may be in such lands or ter-ritories where they can witness and themselves achieve great deeds of arms. And many times Our Lord has favored a number of those who have de-parted in the way I described above both with renown for their great 15

achievements through their physical strength and skill in the good armed combats in which they were engaged so that they drew profit as well as honor from them. And when God has by His grace granted them honor for their great exploits in this military activity, such men deserve to be praised and honored everywhere, provided that they do not, because of the   20 . profits they have made, give up the exercise of arms too soon, for he who too quickly gives it up may easily diminish his reputation. And no one should give up performing great exploits, for when the body can do no more, the heart and determination should take over; and there are many people who have been more fortunate in the end than they had hoped for   25 at the beginning in relation to the nature of their enterprise. I therefore say: whoever does best is worth most.

Deeds Undertaken for Rewards

11   There is another category of men who do not want to leave their own area nor to bear arms for another if they do not reap great rewards before they are willing to depart, and do not want to put any of their own re- sources into the undertaking, even if they have the wherewithal to do so, and contribute little toward the armor. Yet, all the same, when such men   5 are fortunate enough to perform well in this practice of arms in several good battles in the company of those from whom they take their material rewards, these men-at-arms deserve praise for what they have achieved in the good armed combats in which they have participated, thus deserving the material rewards which they have had from this. But I say yet again: he   10 who does best is most worthy.

Deeds Undertaken for Love of a Lady

12   There is another category of men-at-arms who when they begin are so naïve that they are unaware of the great honor that they could win through deeds of arms; nevertheless they succeed so well because they put their hearts into winning the love of a lady. And they are so fortunate that their ladies themselves, from the great honor and superb qualities that re-   5 side in them, do not want to let them tarry nor delay in any way the win- ning of that honor to be achieved by deeds of arms, and advise them on this and then command them to set out and put all their efforts into winning renown and great honor where it is to be sought by valiant men; these ladies urge them on to reach beyond any of their earlier aspirations. Such   10 naïve men-at-arms may nevertheless be so fortunate as to encounter such good adventures that their deeds of prowess and achievements in a number

of places and fields of battle are held to be of great account. And they should be praised and honored, and so also should the noble ladies who have inspired them and through whom they have made their name. And one should indeed honor, serve, and truly love these noble ladies and others whom I hold to be ladies who inspire men to great achievement, and it is thanks to such ladies that men become good knights and men-at-arms. Hence all good men-at-arms are rightly bound to protect and defend the honor of all ladies against all those who would threaten it by word or deed. But I must now return to the kind of men-at-arms who act in the way described above. And again I say: he who does best is most worthy.

Men Who Spend Recklessly to Perform Deeds of Arms

13   I must now speak of another category of men-at-arms who deserve praise for their great determination to put their own resources into the pursuit of opportunities for performing deeds of arms, opportunities often to be found both in their own territory and outside it; they put a great deal into traveling in a more honorable style, for it seems to them that this   5 should enable them to achieve more quickly that goal of great honor for which they strive. When through the grace of God they find opportunities for deeds of arms, they fight as well as good men-at-arms are wont to do. But when it comes to waiting for the best time and season to find occasions for deeds of arms, then it often happens that they have to depart, because   10 of the great state and outward show with which they burden them and the great expenditure to which they choose to commit themselves; hence they cannot stay and wait for the due time and season which they desire so much, and they go away, sad at heart. And there are some who want to put as much in one year as would require a longer stay. It is then a great shame   15 when a good career is held back by excessive spending, for it is better to give an account of how one has been on one's own without a retinue, to take part in armed combats along with other people, and to tell of one's exploits, when God has by his grace granted them, than to say that one lives in such great state and that one has spent too much and has not been able   20 to stay until the right moment. Yet for the great determination that such men have to perform great deeds, which, indeed, they do perform where they have found the opportunity, these men should be esteemed and honored, for that is only right. But because of this, all those who want to establish their reputation should maintain themselves at such a level that they   25 can continue to strive for those achievements which establish them as good men-at-arms. And for this reason it is true that: he who does best is most worthy.

Sacrifices Made by Men-at Arms Whose Deeds Remain Unknown

14   I must now consider yet another category of men-at-arms who deserve praise: that is those who devote a good part of their own financial resources and suffer physical hardship in the search for opportunities for deeds of arms in a number of countries; and they may well find many such opportunities and incur no reproach on many good fields of combat. But it   5 so happens that few learn of their exploits but are only aware of the fact that they have been there, which is in itself a fine thing; for the more one sees great deeds, the more one should learn what is involved and should

talk and take advice at the places where feats of arms are performed or
where one is engaged in other activities. And because of this they deserve   10
to be praised and honored: although their deeds have been of little account,
they have done no ill; for it is very important in such activity to pause and
look. Hence so it is that he who does best is most worthy.

Those Who Are Brave But Too Eager for Plunder

15   I now need to consider yet another category of men-at-arms, who deserve praise, who are strong and skillful, bold and sparing no effort, some
of whom always want to be at the forefront, riding as foragers to win booty
or prisoners or other profit from the enemies of those on whose side they
fight. And they know well how to do it skillfully and cleverly; and because   5
they are so intent on plunder, it often happens that on the entry into a town
won by force, those who are so greedy for plunder dash hither and thither
and find themselves separated from those of their companions who have no
thought for gain but only for completing their military undertaking. And
it often happens that such men, those who ride after and hunt for great   10
booty, are killed in the process—frequently it is not known how, sometimes
by their enemies, sometimes through quarrels in which greed for plunder
sets one man against another. It often occurs that through lack of those
who chase after plunder before the battle is over, that which is thought to
be already won can be lost again and lives or reputations as well. It can also   15
happen in relation to such people who are very eager for booty that when
there is action on the battlefield, there are a number of men who pay more
attention to taking prisoners and other profit, and when they have seized
them and other winnings, they are more anxious to safeguard their captives
and their booty than to help to bring the battle to a good conclusion. And   20
it may well be that a battle can be lost in this way. And one ought instead
to be wary of the booty which results in the loss of honor, life, and possessions. In this vocation one should therefore set one's heart and mind on
winning honor, which endures for ever, rather than on winning profit and
booty, which one can lose within one single hour. And yet one should   25
praise and value those men-at-arms who are able make war on, inflict damage on, and win profit from their enemies, for they cannot do it without
strenuous effort and great courage. But again I shall repeat: he who does
best is most worthy.

How the Highest Standard in Deeds of Arms Is Achieved

16   Having considered all these different forms of the practice of arms,
it is now time to speak of the truest and most perfect form which exists

and is to be found in a number of men-at-arms, as you can learn in what
follows. It is embodied in those who, from their own nature and instinct,
as soon as they begin to reach the age of understanding, and with their   5
understanding they like to hear and listen to men of prowess talk of military
deeds, and to see men-at-arms with their weapons and armor and enjoy
looking at fine mounts and chargers; and as they increase in years, so they
increase in prowess and in skill in the art of arms in peace and in war; and
as they reach adulthood, the desire in their hearts grows ever greater to ride   10
horses and to bear arms. And when they are old enough and have reached
the stage when they can do so, they do not seek advice nor do they believe
anyone who wants to counsel them against bearing arms at the first opportunity, and from that time forward, on more and more occasions; and as
they increase in years, so they increase in prowess and in skill in the art of   15
arms for peace and for war. And they themselves, through their great zeal
and determination, learn the true way to practice the military arts until
they, on every occasion, know how to strive toward the most honorable
course of action, whether in relation to deeds of arms or in relation to other
forms of behavior appropriate to their rank. Then they reflect on, inform   25
themselves, and inquire how to conduct themselves most honorably in
all circumstances. They do this quickly and gladly, without waiting for
admonitions or exhortations. Thus it seems that such men have made a
good reputation for themselves through their own efforts; in this way they
double the good to be found in them, when from their own instinct and   25
the will for good which God has given them, they know what is right
and spare neither themselves nor what they own in their effort to achieve it.
This can be clearly apparent to us in the way that they come forward; for,
at the outset, the first exercise in the use of arms which they can encounter
is jousting, and they are eager to do it. And when God by his grace grants   30
them frequent success in jousting, they enjoy it, and their desire to bear
arms increases. Then after jousting, they learn about the practice of arms in
tournaments, and it becomes apparent to them and they recognize that
tournaments bring greater honor than jousting for those who perform well
there. Then they set out to bear arms in tournaments as often as they can.   35
And when, by God's grace, they perform well there, joyfully, gladly, and
openly, then it seems to them that tournaments contribute more to their
renown and their status than jousting had done; so they no longer take part
in jousts as often as they were wont to do, and go to tournaments instead.
Their knowledge increases until they see and recognize that the men-at-   40
arms who are good in war are more highly prized and honored than any

other men-at-arms. It therefore seems to them from their own observation that they should immediately take up the practice of arms in war in order to achieve the highest honor in prowess, for they cannot attain this by any other form of armed combat. And as soon as they realize this, they give up 45 participating so frequently in exercising their skill at arms in local events and take up armed combat in war. They look around, inquire, and find out where the greatest honor is to be found at that particular time. Then they go to that place and, in keeping with their natural good qualities, are keen to discover all the conditions of armed combat in war, and cannot be satis- 50 fied with themselves if they do not realize to the full their wish to find themselves there and to learn.

How to Study the Art of War

17 They want to observe and to find out how to set up an expedition to attack and fight one's enemies, and to observe the deployment of light horsemen, the deployment of men-at-arms and foot soldiers, and the best way to advance in a fine attack and to make a safe and honorable withdrawal, when it is the time to do so. And when they have observed that, 5 they then will not be content until they have been present at and learned about the defense of castles and walled towns: how they can be held, guarded, and provisioned against both enemy attack and siege, and against all advances against them which can be made; what should be done in relation to an encounter from within. And they still do not want to give up 10 at this point, even though they have achieved great honor in this form of the practice of arms; they always want to learn more because they hear people talk about how one can lay siege to walled towns and castles. Then they do their best to seek out the places where such sieges are going on. And when they come there, they take great pleasure in seeing how a siege 15 is set up to surround the town or castle, how the *battifol* are made to block the way out for the besieged, and to exert more pressure on them, how mining is carried out under the cover of devices such as sows, *buyres*, cats, and belfries, and other matters, such as how to mount an attack on the walls, to climb up on ladders, and to pierce the walls and to enter and take 20 by force. They are then glad when God by his grace has granted that they should have been there, observed, and performed well during this military operation. And the more these men see and themselves perform brave deeds, the more it seems to them, because of the high standards their natural nobility demands of them, that they have done nothing and that they 25 are still only at the beginning. And as a result of this, they are still not satisfied, for they have heard talk as to how one should fight on the battle-field, men-at-arms against others, and they hear those who were there recall the great exploits that good warriors achieved there; then it seems to them that they have seen and done nothing if they do not take part in such a 30 noble form of military activity as a battle. They therefore take pains to travel to different places and to endure great physical hardship in their journeys through many countries across land and sea. And when, through the grace of God, they find out and witness such supremely noble affairs as battles, were they also to be granted the grace and favor of performing great deeds, 35 then such men should indeed thank Our Lord and serve him for the kind-ness he has shown them and the assistance he has given in their continuance of these military pursuits. And when they recognize what a great benefit and honor it is, this increases their determination to strive to seek out op-portunities for such deeds of arms. And when they are fortunate enough to 40 find them, this is very good; and he who is the most fortunate in often taking part in them and in doing his duty well in his own region and in others is of that much greater worth than those who have done less. The question which is the better of two revolves around the honors, of which one is more worthy than the other. Every man who does well in this mili- 45 tary vocation should be prized and honored, and one should observe those who are best and learn by listening to them and by asking about what one does not know, for they ought rightly to know better how to explain, teach, and advise than the others, for they have seen and known, taken part in, experienced, and proved themselves in all forms of armed combat in which 50 good men have learned and learn how to excel. It therefore follows that they should know how to speak about everything that concerns armed combat and many other matters. And in relation to such talk, some might argue over and question which might be the kind of person from whom one might derive the greatest benefit. Would it be the impoverished com- 55 panions who make and have made a name for themselves in the manner explained above, or would it be the great lords who want to make their reputation and have done so in the same way, and are of equal worth in wisdom and in conduct, and in skill and performance in combat? It seems to me that one can give a good answer to this question, for the impover- 60 ished fighting companions rightly deserve esteem and praise, those who with their limited resources set out to make such strenuous efforts and ex-ertions, through which they achieve such noble prowess and such great un-derstanding that the renown of their exploits spreads everywhere, which, up until then, had been held to be of little account, nor would they ever 65 have won this reputation if they had not first had the courage to set about achieving the good deeds of arms spoken of above. And from this honor they gained recognition, rise in status, profit, riches and increase in all benefits. It is, therefore, more necessary for them, in their own interest, to perform and have performed these above-mentioned noble deeds than it is for great lords who have no need to go anywhere to become known, as their rank ensures that they are well known; nor do they need to travel about in order to be served and honored, as their rank entitles them to this; nor can necessity move them to go forth in search of financial gain, for they already have considerable riches. Nor do they have any great need after this to travel abroad in search of pleasure or entertainment, for they can have as much as they want in their own land and territory. One should therefore take far greater account of undertakings involving physical hardship and danger which the great lords are prepared to and do embark on of their own free will without any need to do so other than to achieve personal honor, with no further expectation of any reward for the money and effort which they devote to performing these great deeds of arms; these enterprises should be valued more than those of men who expect some profit or advancement or rise in status as a reward for the honor which they have won or are winning.

The Great Influence of a Valiant Lord

18   If it is thus true that greater account is taken of some, the others are not to be valued less because of this, for there is good in all those who perform great deeds. Nevertheless the great lords may be given higher praise for their valor in a number of worthwhile activities than are the impoverished fighting companions who are sometimes worth as much or more than some great lords. But the reason is that when a great nobleman, lord of extensive lands, is of great worth in the way explained above, as a result he loves and values men of worth all the more for the knowledge he has of the great deeds he has seen them perform. And the other companions, who see that good warriors are honored by the great lords for their prowess, become more determined to attain this level of prowess. Thus you can see that one hundred men skilled in deeds of arms make themselves a name all the sooner through one great and worthy lord than would ten by two poor men of great worth, for the great lord has them in his company and loves, honors, and values them and rewards them, and they respect him, love, honor, and esteem him for the great valor they see in him in addition to the love, honor, and reward that he has bestowed on them. Then they strive to attain greater heights of prowess. And for this reason a

good lord gives new life to the territory under his command, and an unworthy lord reduces to nothing a great part of the resources of his territory,   20
and the impoverished good companion cannot maintain anyone nor reward him. And not so much account is taken of being honored by a valiant
poor man as of a valiant great lord. Nor are the valiant poor men as much
respected and obeyed in time of action as are the great lords; but this does
not mean that the good reputation does not belong to and remain with
those who have earned it, whether rich or poor, and he who does most, the   25
more lasting benefit there remains for him and the more worthy he is.

The Heavy Responsibilities of Men of Rank and Prowess

19   I say therefore that one should honor the great lords and those of
middle rank in whom this prowess is to be found. Ah God! What an honorable and weighty burden to bear! And he who bears such a burden should
fear lest he let it fall, for with great effort and endurance, in fearful danger
and with great diligence, for a long time, stretching over a number of years,   5
he has devoted himself to bearing this responsibility on his shoulders, and
in one brief moment he may fall and lose everything, if God does not grant
him the wisdom and good judgment to know how to keep it safe. So it
must seem to everyone that such people should strive with the utmost diligence to ensure that they suffer no reproach against themselves nor against   10
the bounties God has bestowed on them. And when men of such condition
are in the company of other people, they are held in higher regard than the
rest. Then men prefer to listen to them above all others, for they can talk of
great, important and honorable affairs, and it seems to everyone that they
should and can speak of such matters. Thus they are closely observed as   15
examples of good manners and behavior, whether they are in the company
of great lords who hold them in high regard or in the company of ladies
and damsels who also hold them in high regard; and they are questioned
about their situation, way of life, and conduct. It is not, therefore, the only
virtue of those who bear arms that they carry weapons and perform feats   20
of arms; but, in addition to this, it is necessary that in all the respects mentioned above, in no way can anything dishonorable be perceived nor said
concerning them; for there will be much greater talk and notoriety about
their shortcomings than there would be concerning some one without such
a great reputation. And one should take pleasure in hearing about, listening   25
to, and recounting the good deeds, the great feats, and the admirable utter-
ances of such people who are thus striving to achieve, have achieved, and
have perfected themselves in such knightly qualities, both those who have

now departed from this world and those who are still living. We therefore
learn from the good knights and men-at-arms whose great achievements   30
and honorable deeds of prowess and of valor have been related, described,
and told above and which they have accomplished through suffering great
hardship, making strenuous efforts, and enduring fearful physical perils and
the loss of friends whose deaths they have witnessed in many great battles
in which they have taken part; these experiences have often filled their   35
hearts with great distress and strong emotion. If anyone might want to give
an account of their lives, hard as they have been and still are, for the benefit
of those who want to take up this honorable vocation, their adventures
would take too long to record. However, I want to say a little about the
advice they have to give us according to what they themselves recommend   40
to young men who desire to seek such an honorable life, who love and fear
God and His might, and because of this love and fear will beware of and
refrain from evil deeds. In addition, the above-mentioned good men-at-
arms teach that those who want to achieve this honor should not set their
minds on the pleasures of the palate, neither on very good wine nor on   45
delicious food, for these delights are very out of place at a time when they
are not to be had nor to be found at will, as is usually the case for those who
want to seek such honor; and desire for such things makes it more difficult
for them to endure, and their hearts and bodies find it less easy to bear the
lean fare in food and drink which the quest for such honor requires. A man   50
will be reluctant to risk death who has not learned this, and also a man is
reluctant to abstain from such pleasures of eating and drinking who has
become accustomed to them. One should take no pleasure in such delights;
do not concern yourself with being knowledgeable about good dishes and
fine sauces nor spend too much time deciding which wines are the best,   55
and you will live more at ease. But if it so happens that you find good food
and drink, partake of them gladly and sufficiently but not to excess, for men
of worth say that one should not live in order to eat, but one should eat in
order to live, for no one should eat so much that he is too full, nor drink so
much that he is drunk. And one should do all these things in moderation   60
and so live without too much discomfort. And you have heard it said many
times that the young men who are maintained in the great courts of powerful men make little effort to seek out these great trials, for when they have
dipped their fingers in the sauce of the court, and eaten the choice morsels,
they may be reluctant to give this up. Thus one should not grow sluggish   65
in this way, for the man who for his greedy gullet fails to make a name for
himself, should have all those teeth pulled out, one by one, which do him

so much damage as to lose him the high honor he might have acquired in
his youth. Ah! old age, you should indeed be disconsolate when you find
yourself in the body of one, of whatever rank he may be, who could have   70
achieved so much in his youth, but has done nothing, in relation to what
he can and ought to do according to his rank. And such old age must be
sad, grievous, and shameful in the presence of other men of good standing.
All young men who desire to attain such an honorable status should take
note of this. In addition, the above-mentioned men of good standing tell   75
all those who desire to achieve this honor that they should not concern
themselves too much with nor devote too much attention to any game
where greed might overcome them, such as the game of dice, for it is no
longer a game when it is engaged in through greed for gain. And what
usually happens is that when one thinks one will win another's money, one   80
loses one's own, and there are many who lose three hundred, five hundred,
a thousand *livres*, and more of their money. It would have been better for
them to have given the money thus lost for the service of God or to have
apportioned it to good knights and squires who have already merited such
a gift or would like to merit it; those of high or middle rank who had the   85
the will to give in this way would earn a good reputation. If those would
each according to their power act thus, there would be more good fighting
men than there are now, were they to see that their will for it would be
recognized. However, there are many who take up gambling for greed of
gain or through a fault in behavior or from a dislike of the company of men   90
of good standing. There is also a game called real tennis at which many
people lose and have lost some of their chattels and their inheritance; and
while playing such games, one would not want to see nor meet any men
of good standing for whom it would be necessary to leave the game and
speak to them and keep them company. One should leave playing dice for   95
money to rakes, bawds, and tavern rogues. And if you are determined to
play, do not mind too much about winning, and do not stake too much of
your money lest your game turn to anger. The situation is the same for real
tennis; women have greatly suffered over this, for ball games used to be
women's pastime and pleasure. Yet it should be apparent that the finest   100
games and pastimes that people who seek such honor should never tire of
engaging in would be in the pastimes of jousting, conversation, dancing,
and singing in the company of ladies and damsels as honorably as is possible and fitting, while maintaining in word and deed and in all places their
honor and status. All good men-at-arms ought rightly to behave thus, for   105
in such society and such occupations and pastimes worthy men-at-arms

make a good start, for glances and desire, love, reflection and memory, gaiety of heart and liveliness of body set them off on the right road and provide a beginning for those who would never have known how to per- form and achieve the great and honorable deeds through which good men-   110 at-arms make their name. Such pastimes are finer and more honorable and can bring more benefits than can games of dice, through which one can lose one's possessions and one's honor and all good company. Yet fine games are good where there is no anger, but when tempers rise, it is no longer play. And when one cannot always be in the kind of good company I have   115 described above, which cannot in this honorable vocation last as long as one might wish, one should go and play games, jest, talk, listen, and ask about matters of which one is ignorant in the company of the best people to be found, and it is of benefit often to frequent such society, for there are many, among whom some great lords, who, for the poor company of   120 which they have been fond, and for the bad advice which they have received and believed have thereby been so diminished in heart and in behavior that sometimes they lose their lives or honor or land or the love of their subjects, and it is the same for those of the middle degree, according to their rank. Thus it should appear to everyone that the best pastime of all is to be often   125 in good company, far from unworthy men and from unworthy activities from which no good can come. The men of worth mentioned above also teach us that, although it befits all men of rank to enjoy the sport of hunting with hawk and hound, it is to be understood that one should not fail in any way to put great effort into anything which might improve one's chance of   130 winning an honorable reputation at any moment of the day or night; for the most precious thing there is to lose is time which passes, and cannot be won back nor can it return; and it can happen that such honor is won in an hour which one might fail to find in a year or indeed ever. And for this reason, you who seek to attain this high honor take care that you do not   135 waste time, for you would lose too much thereby. Indeed anyone who wants to attain this high honor, if he retains his physical health and lives for long enough, cannot and should not be excused from achieving it, provided he be willing to do what is required and could do well if he does not hang back; and no one should be held to be excused, unless physically prevented,   140 whether for lack of funds or of the will for it. Therefore, you should know for certain that there is no one who can or should excuse himself from performing well according to his station, some in relation to arms, others in relation to the clerical vocation, others in relation to the affairs of the world. It therefore behooves each person to engage in the appropriate   145 affairs and undertakings, for those who do well in them deserve to be esteemed and praised, each according to his status and according to what he does. Hence no one should be dismayed at the thought of undertaking great deeds, for the above-mentioned men of standing tell us truly that those who have the will to achieve great worth are already on the way to 150 great achievement. And they speak the truth, for because of their great desire to reach and attain that high honor, they do not care what sufferings they have to endure, but turn everything into great enjoyment. Indeed, it is a fine thing to perform great deeds, for those who rise to great achievement cannot rightly grow tired or sated with it; so the more they 155 achieve, the less they feel they have achieved; this stems from the delight they take in striving constantly to reach greater heights. And great good comes from performing these deeds, for the more one does, the less is one proud of oneself, and it always seems that there is so much left to do. Little importance should be attached to those other paltry pastimes which are of 160 so little worth in comparison with those honorable achievements which are so celebrated and renowned, and are of lasting value. And the men of worth also advise you who aim for this great honor that at the beginning of your career you should not, through your too great concern for your own affairs, remain in your own territory, especially as such matters can be dealt with 165 by your own people, for to stay at home would prevent you from achieving your aim; you should hand these affairs over into the charge of your closest friends; and do not feel depressed if your affairs are not so well looked after and do not prosper as well in the charge of others as they would in your charge or that of your own men, if you were there, for this would not be 170 possible; and it is the established custom, for the man who wants to make a fortune before making his reputation may make the fortune, but there will be little heard of his reputation; and the man who desires to make his reputation before his fortune, and God grants him life and health, cannot fail, with God's help, to make his reputation and can in no way fail to get 175 enough wealth, whatever the delay. You should not care about amassing great wealth, for the more worldly goods a man acquires, the more reluctant he is to die and the greater his fear of death; and the more honor a man gains, the less he fears to die, for his worth and honor will always remain, and the worldly goods will disappear, and soon no one will know where 180 they have gone. And be sure of this: whoever wants to establish himself through greed for wealth, he may in the short term make some kind of a name for himself, but in the end greed for wealth will destroy it utterly, for through great greed many evil deeds are committed, and all evil deeds will

run counter to the great honor you should and do desire to win. You must   185
guard against such greed and all other behavior which might stand in the
way of and deflect you from such a noble achievement as winning honor.
These above-mentioned good men-at-arms whom you are so eager to resemble have further lessons to give you, for although the practice of arms is
hard, stressful and perilous to endure, it seems to them that strength of   190
purpose and cheerfulness of heart makes it possible to bear all these things
gladly and confidently, and all this painful effort seems nothing to them,
for they can think of all that can keep them happy in mind and body, provided there are honorable deeds to be done when they should do them.   195
And these people should live loyally and joyfully, and, among other things,
love a lady truly and honorably, for it is the right position to be in for those
who desire to achieve honor. But make sure that the love and the loving
are such that just as dearly as each of you should cherish your own honor
and good standing, so should you guard the honor of your lady above all
else and keep secret the love itself and all the benefit and the honorable   200
rewards you derive from it; you should, therefore, never boast of the love
nor show such outward signs of it in your behavior that would draw the
attention of others. The reason for this is that when such a relationship
becomes known, no good is, in the end, likely to come of it; great difficulties may arise which then bring serious trouble. The greatest pleasure to be   205
derived from love is not to be found in saying "I love so and so" nor in
behaving in such a way that everyone will say: "That man is the lover of
that lady." And there are many who say that they would not want to love
Queen Guinevere if they did not declare it openly or if it were not known.
Such men would prefer it to be said by everyone that they were the accepted   210
lovers of ladies, even if this were not true, than to love and meet with a
favorable response, were this to be kept secret. And this is ill done, for there
is more perfect joy in being secretly in the company of one's lady than one
could have in a whole year, were it to be known and perceived by many.
And we should know for certain that the most secret love is the most lasting   215
and the truest, and that is the kind of love for which one should aim. But
just as one should want to protect the honor of one's lady concerning one's
relationship with her for the sake of the love one has for her, one should
also protect one's own honor for the sake of the honor of one's lady and for
the love she shows to oneself. That means that by your manners, your be-   220
havior, and your personal bearing you should so present yourself that your
renown may be so good, so noble, and so honorable that you and your
great deeds are held in high esteem in your quarters and on the field, espe-

cially in feats of arms in peace and in feats of arms in war where great honor wins recognition. Thus your ladies will and should be more greatly hon- 225 ored when they have made a good knight or man-at-arms of you. And when one could say that a good knight or a good man-at-arms loves a certain lady, where it might be possible for this to be known, greater honor would indeed come to the lady who might have such a love than to those who might choose to waste their time on a paltry wretch, unwilling to take up 230 arms, neither for deeds of arms in peace nor even for deeds of arms in war, when he would have had the physical strength and skill to perform them. And those who love thus and want to love, what honor do they confer on their ladies when it could be said that each one of these loves a miserable wretch? 235

The Lady Who Sees Her Knight Honored

20   Which one of two ladies should have the greater joy in her lover when they are both at a feast in a great company and they are aware of each other's situation? Is it the one who loves the good knight, and she sees her lover come into the hall where all are at table and she sees him honored, saluted, and celebrated by all manner of people and brought to favorable attention 5 before ladies and damsels, knights and squires, and she observes the great renown and the glory attributed to him by everyone? All of this makes the noble lady rejoice greatly within herself at the fact that she has set her mind and heart on loving and helping to make such a good knight or good man-at-arms. And when she also sees and understands that, in addition to 10 the true love for one another which they share, he is in addition loved, esteemed, and honored by all, this makes her so glad and happy for the great worth to be found in the man who loves her, that she considers her time to have been well spent. And if one of the other ladies loves the miserable wretch who, for no good reason, is unwilling to bear arms, she will 15 see him come into that very hall and perceive and understand that no one pays him any attention or shows him honor or notices him, and few know who he is, and those who do think nothing of him, and he remains hidden behind everyone else, for no one brings him forward. Indeed, if there is such a lady, she must feel very uneasy and disconsolate when she sees that 20 she has devoted time and thought to loving and admiring a man whom no one admires or honors, and that they never hear a word said of any great deed that he ever achieved. Ah God! what small comfort and solace is there for those ladies who see their lovers held in such little honor, with no excuse except lack of will! How do such people dare to love (*amer par amours*) 25

when they do not know nor do they want to know about the worthy deeds that they should know about and ought to perform, especially those who for good reason should undertake them? And indeed this love can be worth nothing, nor can it last for long without the ladies wanting to have no more of it and withdrawing, and the miserable wretches, through   30 well justified shame, dare not protest, nor insist that their ladies should not treat them thus; instead they themselves retreat, and they have to do so in great shame and discomfort, nor can they put forward any arguments to persuade their ladies to behave differently. Therefore men should love secretly, protect, serve, and honor all those ladies and damsels who inspire   35 knights, men-at-arms, and squires to undertake worthy deeds that bring them honor and increase their renown. And these noble ladies should, as is their duty, love and honor these worthy men-at-arms who, in order to deserve their noble love and their benevolence, expose themselves to so much physical danger as the vocation of arms requires from those who aim to   40 reach and achieve that high honor through which they hope to deserve to win the love of their ladies. And the advice of these noble ladies is as follows: "Love loyally if you want to be loved." Thus you should love loyally and live joyfully and act honorably and in good hope, for these activities

of love and of arms should be engaged in with the true and pure gaiety of   45
heart which brings the will to achieve honor.

A Good Man-at-Arms Should Not Pamper His Body

21   Having examined all these different ways of loving, the aforementioned men of worth tell you that you must in no way indulge in too great
fondness for pampering your body, for love of that is the worst kind of
love there is. But instead direct your love toward the preservation of your
soul and your honor, which last longer than does the body, which dies   5
just as soon, whether it be fat or lean. Too great a desire to cosset the body
is against all good. In the first place, if you have this bad tendency for
being excessively fond of cosseting this wretched body in your youth, you
will want to go to sleep early and wake up late, and if your long hours
of sleep are interrupted, you will suffer greatly from this, and the longer   10
you sleep the less time you will have to acquire knowledge and to learn
something of value. And this life of long sleeping will stand in the way of
those who want to attain high honor, for they have often to go to sleep late
and rise early, and they have accustomed themselves to doing so, and this
helps them to achieve physical fitness and honor. The pampering of these   15
wretched bodies also requires white sheets and soft beds, and if these are
sometimes lacking, such men's backs and ribs ache so much that they can
do nothing all day. And these good beds encourage rest and an abundance
of sleep, which prevents them from hearing much that would be of profit
to them. The contrary is true of those who seek honor, for more often than   20
not they have poor beds and many a time they sleep without beds at all and
with their clothes on; and this rest and repose is quite enough for them, for
they would not want it otherwise for the great profit and honor they expect
to have from it. And in addition, to sustain these wretched men's bodies,
which have little time to live, they have to be provided with the best food   25
and wine that are to be found, and require to eat at the right time, or otherwise they will be in too great distress because of the great delight they
take in such things. And because of this gluttony, they dread the hardship
associated with deeds of arms. And indeed such delights are rejected by
those who go in search of this high honor, for they have no regard for and   30
do not indulge in such pleasures, but drink and eat whatever small amount
they find and are quite satisfied; they do so gladly and joyfully for the sake
of the honor which brings them such a great reward; and the men of worth
accept the benefits and the honors which God has bestowed and continues
to bestow on them instead of on the miserable wretches who, as they see,   35

receive nothing. Hence we can learn from the above-mentioned men of worth that it is not good just to live, but to live in a good way. Furthermore those wretched men have to be sustained and pampered so that in winter they are wrapped in furs and warmly clad and live in warm houses, and in summer are lightly clad and live in cool houses or in the coldest vaults,   40 otherwise they cannot survive because of their decadent habits.

Good Men-at-Arms Have No Fear of Discomfort

22   It is quite the opposite for those who want to win honor, for they adapt to the seasons: when it is cold, they endure the cold, and when it is hot, they put up with the heat. And they are prepared to accept all this for the great pleasure they experience in winning honor and in living honorably. And in relation to this we learn from the above-mentioned men of   5 worth that honor is not achieved through spending much time in keeping the body delightfully comfortable. And on top of all these things, it also arises that in order to maintain these wretched bodies, because of their great fear lest they lack their accustomed comforts, they are eager to grab whatever they can whenever they can, and are so miserly in spending that   10 they will only shell out to maintain their bodies in comfort, at which the devils will rejoice. And this is quite the opposite to those who want to spend what they have in winning honor; for they gather together as much as they can of what they have and they make considerable borrowings, so that they owe a great deal on their return, and they are eager to come   15 quickly to a place where they can quickly spend what they have in striving to win honor. And we learn from the above-mentioned men of worth that the practice of arms always gives back what is put in it whatever the delay. And these wretched people are so afraid of dying that they cannot overcome their fear. As soon as they leave their abode, if they see a stone jutting out   20 of the wall a little further than the others, they will never dare to pass beneath it, for it would always seem to them that it would fall on their heads. If they come to a river which is a little big or too fast flowing, it always seems to them, so great is their fear of dying, that they will fall into it. If they cross a bridge which may seem a little too high or too low, they dis-   25 mount and are still terrified lest the bridge collapse under them, so great is their fear of dying. If they see before them a boggy stretch, they will go a good half league out of their way to find some firm ground for fear of sinking into the mud. If they suffer from a slight illness, they think they are about to die. If they are threatened by anyone, they fear greatly for their   30 physical safety and dread the loss of the riches they have amassed in such a

discreditable way. And if they see anyone with a wound, they dare not look
at it because of their feeble spirit. What is more, no matter how strong the
place these poor wretches may find in which to spend the night, if there is
a little too much wind, they will be greatly afraid that the roof will come   35
down on them. Furthermore, when these feeble wretches are on horseback,
they do not dare to use their spurs lest their horses should start to gallop,
so afraid are they lest their horses should stumble and they should fall to
the ground with them. Now you can see that these wretched people who
are so fainthearted will never feel secure from living in greater fear and   40
dread of losing their lives than do those good men-at-arms who have exposed themselves to so many physical dangers and perilous adventures in
order to achieve honor; for they are so accustomed to and familiar with
such things that they are quite unaffected by such pathetic fears to which
these wretches are so often subject. And while the cowards have a great   45
desire to live and a great fear of dying, it is quite the contrary for the men
of worth who do not mind whether they live or die, provided that their life
be good enough for them to die with honor. And this is evident in the
strange and perilous adventures which they seek. For this reason the above-
mentioned men of worth say that a man is happy to die when he finds life   50
pleasing, for God is gracious toward those who find their life of such quality
that death is honorable; for the said men of worth teach you that it is better
to die than to live basely.

Advice on Conduct Toward Friends and Enemies

23   There is a supreme rule of conduct required in these good men-at-
arms as the above-mentioned men of worth inform us: they should be
humble among their friends, proud and bold against their foes, tender and
merciful toward those who need assistance, cruel avengers against their
enemies, pleasant and amiable with all others, for the men of worth tell you   5
that you should not converse at any length nor hold speech with your enemies, for you should bear in mind that they do not speak to you for your
own good but to draw out of you what they can use to do you the greatest
harm. You should be generous in giving where the gift will be best used
and as careful as you can that you let your enemies have nothing that   10
is yours. Love and serve your friends, hate and harm your enemies, relax
with your friends, exert yourself with all your strength against your foes.
You should plan your enterprises cautiously and you should carry them out
boldly. Therefore the said men of worth tell you that no one should fall into
despair from cowardice nor be too confident from great daring, for falling   15

into too great despair can make a man lose his position and his honor, and
trusting too much in his daring can make a man lose his life foolishly; but
when one is engaged on an armed enterprise, one should dread vile cowardice more than death. Take care not to be so greedy as to take what
belongs to others without good cause. And be sure that, as you value your-   20
self, you do not let anything of yours be taken from you. Speak of the
achievements of others but not of your own, and do not be envious of
others. Above all, avoid quarrels, for a quarrel with one's equal is dangerous, a quarrel with some one higher in rank is madness, and a quarrel with
some one lower in rank is a vile thing, but a quarrel with a fool or a drunk   25
is an even viler thing. The aforesaid men of worth also tell you to refrain
from saying unpleasant things and to make sure that what you say is of
some profit rather than merely courteous. And make sure that you do not
praise your own conduct nor criticize too much that of others. Do not desire to take away another's honor, but, above all else, safeguard your own.   30
Be sure that you do not despise poor men or those lesser in rank than you,
for there are many poor men who are of greater worth than the rich. Take
care not to talk too much, for in talking too much you are sure to say something foolish; for example, the foolish cannot hold their peace, and the wise
know how to hold their peace until it is time to speak. And be careful not   35
to be too guileless, for the man who knows nothing, neither of good nor of
evil, is blind and unseeing in his heart, nor can he give himself or others
good counsel, for when one blind man tries to lead another, he himself will
fall first into the ditch and drag the other in after him. Refrain from remon-
strating with fools, for you will be wasting your time, and they will hate   40
you for it; but remonstrate with the wise, who will like you the better for
it. Do not put too much faith in people who have risen rapidly above others
by good fortune, not merit, for this will not last: they can fall as quickly as
they rise. And the aforementioned men of worth tell you that fortune tests
your friends, for when it abandons you, it leaves you those who are your   45
friends and takes away those who are not. I repeat that you should never
regret any generosity you may show and any gifts well bestowed, for the
above-mentioned men of worth tell you that a man of worth should not
remember what he has given except when the recipient brings the gift back
to mind for the good return he makes for it. You must avoid acquiring a   50
bad reputation for miserliness in your old age, for the more you have given,
the more you should give, for the longer you have lived, the less time you
will have yet to live. And above all refrain from enriching yourself at others'
expense, especially from the limited resources of the poor, for unsullied

poverty is worth more than corrupt wealth. The aforementioned men of   55
worth also tell you that you should treat your friends in such a way that you
have no need to fear lest they become your enemies, for you should consider that as long as you keep your secret to yourself, it is always within
your control, but as soon as you have revealed it, you are at its mercy. And
if you have to reveal it, only disclose it to your loyal friend, and disclose   60
your illness only to a loyal doctor. The aforementioned men of worth also
tell you that when moving against your enemies to meet them in battle,
never admit the idea that you might be defeated nor think how you might
be captured or how you might flee, but be strong in heart, firm, and confident, always expecting victory, not defeat, whether or not you are on top,   65
for whatever the situation, you will always do well because of the good
hopes that you have. Indeed, many retreat when, if they had stayed and
done what they could, their enemies might have been defeated; and some
who have been easily taken prisoner, if they had resisted as well as they
could, their enemies would have suffered great losses. You should, there-   70
fore, always and in all circumstances be determined to do your best, and
above all have the true and certain hope that comes from God that He will
help you, not relying just on your strength nor your intelligence nor your
power but on God alone, for one often sees that the best men are defeated
by lesser men, and a greater number of people may be defeated by a smaller,   75
and the strongest in body may be overcome by the weakest, and the wisest
and best ordered in battle by the most foolish and worst ordered. You can
see clearly and understand that you on your own can achieve nothing except what God grants you. And does not God confer great honor when He
allows you of His mercy to defeat your enemies without harm to yourself?   80
And if you are defeated, does not God show you great mercy if you are
taken prisoner honorably, praised by friends and enemies? And if you are
in a state of grace and you die honorably, does not God show you great
mercy when He grants you such a glorious end to your life in this world
and bears your soul away with Him into eternal bliss? And you can see that   85
no one should be too afraid or too overjoyed or too disturbed at such hap-
penings when they occur, but should give thanks and commit everything
into the hands of Him who gives graciously more than one can ask for. And
the aforesaid men of worth teach you that if you want to be strong and of
good courage, be sure that you care less about death than about shame.   90
And those who put their lives in danger with the deliberate intention of
avoiding shame are strong in all things. The aforesaid men of worth also
tell you that you should reflect in your hearts on the things which may

happen to you, both the good and the bad, so that you can suffer the bad patiently and treat the good with restraint. And in all adversity be always 95 steadfast and wise. And you also need to consider how you can and must maintain any benefit or honor which God may bestow on you, so that you do not lose them through negligence such as by removing yourself and distancing yourself from trouble when it comes upon you; and you should first thank and praise Him who gives you these things and preserve 100 them without arrogance, for you must understand that where there is arrogance, there reigns anger and all kinds of folly; and where humility is to be found, there reigns good sense and happiness. And as the aforesaid men of worth teach you and tell you truly, if arrogance were to be so high that it towered up into the clouds and its highest point reached the heavens, it 105 would have to fall and would crumble and be reduced to nothing. And you should know that from arrogance grow many branches from which many evils come, so many as may cause the loss of soul and body, honor and wealth. You should preserve what you know and the honor you have without arrogance. And what you do not know, you should ask with due hu- 110 mility to be taught it. The aforesaid men of worth also tell you not to put too much trust in the gifts of fortune, for they are things which are destined to come to an end, whether through loss or illness or force or death, for death spares no one, neither the high nor the low, but levels all. And no one therefore should delay, because such gifts do not last for long, but can 115 vanish at any moment, without waiting for the hour. And the man who perfectly understands this will never be overcome by arrogance.

The Role of Fortune

24   And because the benefits of fortune have been discussed above, and some may not understand what these are, it is necessary to give a brief explanation of them so that people have a better knowledge of them and understand better the position of fortune in this calling. And in relation to this, it could be said that one should not put trust in the benefits of fortune, 5 which are not earned, for fortune is fickle and is destined to come to an end. But if you have the will to be wise and you strive at it, and in return for your efforts God, through His grace, grants you wisdom, and through this you are exalted, this benefit does not come from fortune: it should last, 10 provided you know how to preserve it honestly, in controlling yourself first, and then others if necessary. For if you are wise, you will only do good and ought not to excuse yourself from being a man of worth and loyal, as it is the greatest and most supreme good there is, for a man may want to be

wise and fail, and want to be valiant and fail, and want to be rich and powerful and fail, but no one should or can excuse himself from being a man of   15
worth and loyal, if he has the will. And if you have the reputation of being
a good man-at-arms, through which you are exalted and honored, and you
have deserved this by your great exertions, by the perils you have faced and
by your courage, and Our Lord has in his mercy allowed you to perform
the deeds from which you have gained such a reputation, such benefits are   20
not benefits of fortune, but are benefits which by right should last, provided
that one knows how to conserve them humbly and honorably. And it often
happens, as has been said earlier, that in armed encounters in battle the
smaller number defeats the greater, and many a time the worst marshaled
on the field defeat those who are well marshaled, and many a time the lesser   25
and weaker have defeated those who were in every respect greater and the
nobler in rank. This fortune is good, for the great prowess and valor which
in those battles is to be found in the victors; and for the faintheartedness of
the conquered and defeated whom they have overcome in relation to these
battles, it could be called ill fortune for the vanquished and worse fortune   30
for those who themselves caused the defeat. Nevertheless if the lesser number encounter the greater number, and the weaker the stronger, and the ill
marshaled those who are well marshaled, and they wanted to continue thus
for some length of time, this run of good fortune would not last long
without changing for the worse, and this is according to reason. Reason   35
is always more certain and assured and long lasting, for there is no good
fortune which may not at any moment be changed and brought down
to earth. And if, by your great worth and your good sense or by your
strenuous efforts, you have done good and honorable service, however low
you may be in rank, if you are raised to a noble and high rank in possessions   40
and other advantages of this world, these benefits which have come to you
by the grace of God are not the gifts of fortune. They should retain their
value and last as long as the benefits of this world can last, provided you
safeguard them and put them to proper use, finding no great glory in them
except in relation to God who has given them to you. These benefits, thus   45
well merited and put to good and careful use, without arrogance, without
damage to others, without indulgence in greed or excessive pleasure, are all
benefits that can be justified. But those who are reputed to be wise and are
not, and those who are reputed to be men of worth and are not, and those
who are reputed to have won honor through deeds of arms and are un-   50
worthy of this renown, and those who have been raised up to noble rank
and great wealth and high estate, when people of that kind are elevated to

such good fortune, they know no better than to exploit this with very little restraint. As a result, the foundation on which their height of fortune is based is so weak that it must crumble and collapse so that they come 55 tumbling down those very steps which they had earlier mounted; they, therefore, suffer more from the descent through having mounted so high. Hence the proverb of the ancients is true: "He that climbs higher than he should falls lower than he would." You see, therefore, that the benefits which are well earned and well deserved are those which, according to rea- 60 son, should reach the greatest perfection and last, be they of the soul or of the body; and those who want to have the great benefits and honors without painful effort, and in idleness take all their ease and pleasure, such people, however long they wait, will get nothing. And because of this, there is no one, however humble or of however low a rank, if he is willing to 65 strive for and deserve honorable achievement, to whom the benefits may not come in such abundance that he could not ask for more and to whom God may not grant together with these things an honorable reputation. Nor are there any men so important or of such high rank that they will win any of the rewards if they cannot endure the great effort required from 70 those who would deserve to have such benefits; rather they will remain inadequate, out of favor with the people and with a bad reputation, for the more a man is of high and noble rank, the more his reputation, whether good or bad, will spread throughout the world, more than would be the case for many of middle rank. If anyone would like to know why and how 75 the emperors, kings and princes of lands were raised up and made lords over their people, the reasons for doing this and the way it was done were good, holy and just; for the persons with the best physical qualities and the highest standard of moral conduct, selected from among all the people, these men chose them at that time; from these descended the emperors, 80 kings, and princes of today. And do you think that those above-mentioned who were the first to be selected, were chosen to be lords to take their ease and their pleasure? Indeed no! Were they chosen because they did not love God and his works and the Holy Church? Indeed no! Were they chosen to harm the common people and to obtain profit for themselves? Indeed 85 no! Were they created to impoverish their people and enrich themselves without good cause? Indeed no! Were they created to have power and riches and to make ill use of them? Indeed no! Were they created not to maintain justice for the humble as well as for the great? Indeed no! Were they created to be cruel, without pity and without mercy? Indeed no! 90 Were they created to linger for a long time in idleness and to make little effort? Indeed no! Were they created so that they might eat and drink as luxuriously as they could? Indeed no! Were they chosen in order to refrain from taking up arms and from exposing themselves to the perils of battle in the defense of their lands and people? Indeed no! Were they chosen in order 95 to be cowards? Indeed no! Were they chosen to be miserly and not give to those who deserve it? Indeed no! Were they chosen to lead dishonest and ill famed lives? Indeed no! Were they elected to be generous to the unworthy and to bestow gifts on wastrels? Indeed no! Were they chosen to cherish and believe in the unworthy and the flatterers? Indeed no! Were 100 they chosen in order to send away from their company men of worth? Indeed no! Were they chosen to shut themselves up in their houses where no one can speak to them? Indeed no! Were they chosen to lie and to break their promises, oaths, and sealed agreements? Indeed no! Were they chosen to commit, have others commit, or give consent to any misdeed? Indeed 105 no! Were they chosen to have any pleasant relations or friendship with those who lead a wicked life? Indeed no! Were they chosen in order to take pleasure in listening to dissolute conversation or in watching worthless pastimes? Indeed no! Were they chosen in order to take pleasure in listening to malicious comments on others in their presence? Indeed no! Were they 110 chosen so that when they meet adversity they cannot endure it or bear it? Indeed no! Were they chosen in order to be proud, arrogant, and cruel to those who serve them? Indeed no! Were they chosen in order to go and take their pleasure in sports of the woods and rivers instead of undertaking their great tasks? Indeed no! Were they chosen to be whoremongers or fre- 115 quenters of taverns? Indeed no! Were they chosen so that they could despise and disdain poor men? Indeed no! Were they chosen in order to curse or blaspheme wickedly against God or the Virgin Mary or the saints? Indeed no! Were they chosen in order to be idle and to do nothing? Indeed no! Were they chosen so that they could not and would not speak to those who 120 approach them? Indeed no!

The True Function for Which Rulers Were Created

25   Now, after all these questions and answers, we must come to the true explanation for the creation of such emperors, kings, and princes of great lands and peoples. You should know that at that time were chosen those who were seen to have good physique, strong, and well equipped to endure hardship of all kinds and to strive for the good government of their people, 5 whether in time of war or of peace. These personages and these lords were not raised up to have great periods of rest nor great pleasures nor great

delights, but to endure more and to strive harder than any of the others.
And in relation to the persons chosen as explained above, they were examined and questioned and interrogated diligently concerning their qualities   10
in order to discover whether they were fit persons to govern the people, and
then they were chosen. You should know that they were chosen in order to
endure and withstand greater physical hardship, painful exertions, and
mental anxiety than any of their people because of the heavy responsibility
they had taken on in the task of government for which they had been cho-   15
sen and with which they had been entrusted. They showed then great diligence in giving their people good government, and they were chosen that
they might love, fear, and serve God and all his works. They were, therefore, chosen so that they might place the people's profit before their own.
They were, therefore, chosen that they might protect their people without   20
taking anything from them apart from those dues the people owed to their
lord, and it was not for the lords to enrich themselves at the cost of impov-
erishing the people without reasonable cause. They were, therefore, chosen
to spend their wealth on all kinds of good works so that they were not
reproached for making ill use of it. They were, therefore, chosen to admin-   25
ster justice and to maintain the rights of the humble as well as of the
mighty. They were, therefore, chosen that they might show pity and mercy
where appropriate. They were, therefore, chosen that they might avoid
long stays in one place and to exert themselves for the good of their common people. They were, therefore, chosen to be the first to take up arms   30
and to strive with all their might and expose themselves to the physical
dangers of battle in defence of their people and their land. They were, therefore, chosen to be bold and of good courage against their enemies and
against all those who seek to deprive them of possessions or honor. They
were, therefore, chosen to give of their own freely and generously to men   35
of worth who had well deserved it and to those likely to deserve it and to
the poor to sustain them. They were, therefore, chosen to be careful and
to conserve what they have without giving or distributing it to unworthy
people nor to those of poor standing nor for the committing of evil deeds.
They were, therefore, chosen so that they might lead lives of such integrity   40
that no reproach could be levelled against them, nor could they be held in
ill repute for any unworthy or shameful behavior; for their good and honest
way of life should set an example for others. They were, therefore, chosen
so that they might drive away from their company all worthless people,
all liars and flatterers, and all others of a base disposition, and to avoid all   45
association with them. They were, therefore, chosen to love, honor, and

hold dear the good and the wise and the men of worth, to pay heed to their words, to associate closely with them and enjoy their company. They were, therefore, chosen to show themselves often and to move among the people, to listen often and to give replies concerning matters which may affect 50 themselves and others, and sometimes to disport themselves with their own men. They were, therefore, chosen in order to keep their spoken promises, and so, for even stronger reasons, they should keep their sworn and sealed undertakings and never declare them null and void. They were, therefore, chosen that they might keep away from themselves and their company all 55 men of ill repute and evil way of life and to take no pleasure in them. They were, therefore, chosen that they might take no delight in hearing any shameful words or in playing or watching any worthless games. They were, therefore, chosen so that their nobility would not tolerate the slandering of others, neither men nor women, nor the speaking ill of people without 60 good cause. They were, therefore, chosen so that when they encountered adversity or persecution, they should know how to endure and bear them wisely and valiantly and with great courage. They were, therefore, chosen, so that when they are at the height of their power and lordship and at the time of their great victories over their enemies, they would know how to 65 behave in this position, with due humility and without arrogance, and showing mercy, without excessive pride and ferocity, giving thanks and ac- knowledging their indebtedness for all that they have to God from whom they hold it and who gave it to them and who can take everything away from them again whenever it may please Him. They were, therefore, chosen 70 so that, when participating in or watching the pleasure of the chase, with hawk or hound, in the woods or by the river, however much they might enjoy these sports and take delight in them, that this should not lead them to neglect neither for a day nor even an hour the duties required to maintain good government both on their own behalf and on that of their people. 75 They were, therefore, chosen so that they should not visit nor frequent dis- reputable places such as brothels and taverns, for they are not places in which great lords should let it be seen that they take pleasure, for the sake of their own good reputation and in order not to incite disreputable behav- ior, for many might want to follow the example set by the great lords in 80 relation to such places. They were, therefore, chosen so that they should not despise any poor people, whether men or women, nor disdain to listen to them, and should treat them more benevolently than they would treat richer men; for they have not the same means to carry on their affairs as have the richer men, and as a result, many poor men, on account of their 85

lack of financial means, have failed to achieve by their lengthy endeavors what by right they should have done. They were, therefore, chosen so that they should in no way use bad language nor curse in the name of Our Lord or that of the Virgin Mary or those of the saints, for the higher their rank the more they should make sure that God be feared, loved, served and hon-   90
ored in word and deed wherever they are. They were, therefore, chosen that there might be no idleness in them, lest they might not always devote all their thoughts and efforts to striving on behalf of themselves and their people. They were, therefore, chosen so that they might know how to speak and respond adequately in relation to what is asked or requested of them.   95

The Good Rulers Contrasted with the Unworthy

26   Now you can perceive and know by the qualities set out above which are the good and which are the unworthy princes, for those who have more of these qualities are superior to the others; and those who have less are to that degree inferior; and those who have more bad characteristics than good are not worthy to hold land or govern people; and the same can   5
be said of other lords such as dukes, counts, barons, and others of whatever rank, in relation to ruling over great lands and peoples. And it can also be said of all nobles, be they only of middle rank: he who does best will he not always be the most praised, esteemed, and honored? And is it not very strange that there are those who prefer to do evil and lead vile lives and   10
do vile deeds rather than good ones? Surely, ill deeds are shameful, fearful, and dangerous to commit, and unworthy ways of life bring shame, blame, and an increase of sin, and unworthy acts lead to behaving in a shameful and dishonorable way in relation to worthy men, bringing one to a bad end. It should, therefore, be recognized firmly and with certainty that   15
deeds of valor, a good way of life, and good undertakings are more pleasant to carry out than are the above-mentioned bad ones; for those who perform deeds of valor do so gladly, confidently and without fear of reproach; and those who lead a good life can fittingly go anywhere freely and without fear. Those who carry out noble undertakings should take no account of envy or   20
hatred of which they may be the object or of any ill which may be said of them or which people may want to do to them; for their deeds of valor, way of life and noble undertakings will bear them along, direct them, and keep them safe everywhere. And the same could be said by anyone who might want to speak of the princes and prelates of the Holy Church such as   25
popes, cardinals, patriarchs, archbishops, bishops, priests, and other ministers of the Holy Church who have the care of souls, but it does not befit

lay people to speak more of this, rather they should hold their peace as best they can.

The Scale of Qualities in a Man of Worth: Simplicity of Heart

27   Now I have described to you above the way of life, the qualities and conduct of great princes and other lords, including those of middle rank, in which each person of whatever degree should strive to achieve the very highest standard so that they will be of greater worth and will live more happily and honorably. There might, then, be some persons who, for one   5
or two good qualities which they might have, might think and believe that these will suffice for them and that it would not matter about the rest, and it is therefore right that the good exploits that should be performed by those people who want to achieve honor at arms should finally be described a little more clearly in order that it should be known what they are. You   10
can and ought to know that the best qualities that anyone can aim for and achieve is to be a man of worth, according to what is required to attain this completely. As for declaring some one to be a man of worth, there are some whom one can well hold to be men of worth for their pure simplicity of heart, and they would scarcely know how to do wrong, even if they wanted   15
to do so, for they are themselves so innocent. And because good actions are easier to do and to control than are evil ones, these simple people set out to perform them all; all the same, in doing this they behave wisely, for it is better to hold to the good. Yet there may be greater virtues in some than are to be found in these aforementioned simple people.   20

Those Who Present Themselves Outwardly as Generous and Devout

28   Some may be held to be in a different way men of worth, that is those who give alms freely and like to be in church and attend mass frequently and say many paternosters and other prayers and fast in Lent and other recommended fasts. But perhaps there are in some of those men less obvious characteristics opposed to the good qualities mentioned above: for ex-   5
ample, there may be concealed in their hearts greed or envy of others or hatred or ill will or many other things that detract from a great part of the good characteristics mentioned above. They are held to be men of worth for the characteristics which are apparent in them, but nevertheless one can do better as far as being a man of worth is concerned.   10

Those Who Act Loyally and Serve God

29   And there are those who should be held to be men of worth by everyone. That is those who love, serve, and honor God and His gentle Mother and all His power, and refrain from actions by which they might incur Their wrath, and who have within them such steadfast qualities that their way of life cannot be criticized for any vile sins nor for any shameful re- 5 proach, and they thus live loyally and honestly. And these should be held to be men of worth. Thus some could be considered wise who are very clever, but they direct their intelligence to such malicious ends that they lose the true and natural good sense which men ought and should know how to use were they to have the will to do so, but they set their intelligence to work 10 toward evil rather than good; nevertheless intelligence is needed to perform such evil deeds, but it is not good to have knowledge combined with such intentions.

Those Who Are Too Ingenious and Over Subtle

30   And there are others whom some consider to be wise, but they put all their intelligence and concentrated effort into such cunning schemes that their great subtlety sometimes turns them aside from reaching a true, loyal, and sensible conclusion, so that these subtle people are out of step in all undertakings. Like those who leave the good main road to follow minor 5 paths and then get lost, in the same way, through their great subtlety they fail to act according to natural good sense, and therefore they will not profit fully from their natural intelligence through setting their mind to such great subtlety.

Those Who Are Truly Wise

31   And there are some whom everyone should consider to be wise. It is those who, from their youth, strive diligently to learn what is best to do, to distinguish good from evil, and to know what is reasonable to do; and because they recognize what course of action would be against reason, they endeavor to behave loyally, confidently, and according to what is right. And 5 in their dealings with others, such people do not seek to take away the rights of others, but want above all to protect such rights for them and their honor as well. And in addition, these people know well how to advise others honestly and wisely, without any evil malice, not using excessive subtlety, and without incurring shameful reproach. These should be held 10 to be truly wise, and such power of reasoning is good if it is always put to good use.

Those Who Have Courage and Skill But Are Thoughtless

32   Now it is time to speak of those good men-at-arms who are held to be valiant, of whom there are some who are skilled in handling weapons,

brave, and adept, but their way of pursuing a career in arms is always such
that when they are in action, they do not consider the benefit or advantage
for their friends or the harm done to their enemies, but, without giving or   5
taking advice, they spur forward in a disorderly way and perform personally
many feats of arms. This is often more to their disadvantage than to their
advantage, but they achieve many striking deeds of arms, and in this way
take part in many good battles without attempting to contribute in any
other way, but they cannot be reproached in relation to the honor earned   10
through bravery; and these men, who have seen so many great days of combat and made such a fine contribution by their physical exploits, should
indeed be called worthy, although as for being worthy in the truest sense,
it would be possible to do better.

Those Who Perform Great Deeds But Do Not Lead or Advise

33   There are yet other good men-at-arms who should be held to be worthy. That is those who have gone in search of military undertakings in many
places, in distant lands and foreign parts, and have found them where another is in command, so that they have no responsibilities of leadership,
and they have not involved themselves much in leading or in giving advice,   5
but have undertaken whatever fighting has presented itself to them in an
honorable way and without reproach. Nevertheless, when, through God's
grace, they have been given the opportunity for so much strenuous effort
and for so many good days of combat where they can win honor, they
should be held to be worthy, although in relation to such a standard of   10
prowess, one might do better.

The True Men of Worth, Brave and of Good Counsel

34   There are yet others who should above all men be held to be of great
worth. That is those who in their youth, in the places and the battles in
which they have taken part, have risked their lives gladly and boldly and
without any thought or fear of death, of prison, or of the expense which
might be incurred in seeking these adventures, for too much good sense is   5
not right for young men at the beginning of their career in arms. And when
these young men learn what the practice of arms involves or what it can
mean in terms of both honor and danger, these good men-at-arms acquire
wisdom and understanding which lead to full knowledge. And through the
great knowledge that these men have gained from the adventures they en-   10
countered in their youth and through what they learned and remembered
from their experiences, they begin to act wisely on their own behalf when

the need arises in their wars, and all goes well for them because of their
good sense and the way they know how to conduct themselves; they also
know well how to help and counsel others in their wars. And these good   15
men in whom is to be found so much experience and bravery in the practice
of arms are entrusted with the command of men-at-arms to lead them in
combat as captains, constables, and marshals or in other offices concerned
with the direction of the practice of arms. The quality of these good men-
at-arms has been thus fully proved through their great physical exploits,   20
through their strenuous efforts of endurance, through their good sense and
wise counsel, through their great acts of true valor and their fine words,
which are indeed fitting in relation to such deeds, through their splendid
bearing, to be seen under the very difficult conditions often to be encountered in the practice of arms, whether winning or losing, through the great   25
support which should and is to be found in them in all situations, and
finally through the absence of any characteristics which could under any
circumstances be criticized or condemned. And these are the good men-
at-arms who have sought out and experienced many fine adventures and
battles, in which they always acquit themselves with great honor, receiving   30
universal praise from friend and foe alike. It is from such as these that those
men of worth are made who surpass those who have been spoken of before,
for often to seek out good days of battle and often to perform with great
honor serve to provide evidence for all to see of the valor of those who
prove their worth there, for the fine proofs of valor which these excellent   35
men-at-arms have furnished in many good days in the pursuit of arms give
them this renown for prowess, for which everyone should consider them
to be men of worth, the most glorious name to win in the practice of arms.
And these men are to be prized and honored above all the other men of
prowess described above.   40

The Men-at-Arms of Supreme Worth

35   After this examination of all these good qualities and achievements
described above, it is now time to speak of another category of men who
are and ought to be supreme among all lay people. These are men who are
rightly said to be of high merit, and are more honored, better loved and
prized than any other men-at-arms. And in order better to learn about the   5
men of high merit, one needs to know how and why they should be held in
such high esteem. You should know that if a man were sufficiently intelli-
gent but not a man of worth, his intelligence would be turned wholly to
evil. And if a man were of worth and had not enough wisdom, he would

still be of merit, but not of such value and of such merit as the wise men of   10
natural good sense who are true men of worth. And as for having a reputation for prowess without being a man of worth or wise, do not expect in
the end any great perfection in such prowess. For this reason, if you know
of some one who is endowed with the gift of the kind of intelligence presented as the best of the three kinds of intelligence described above, and   15
you know that in this person is also to be found all the qualities of a man
of worth, the very best of the three kinds of worth, as mentioned above,
and you know that in addition there is in this man true and loyal prowess,
of the best of the three kinds described above, so that this man and others
like him combine within themselves throughout their lives these three su-   20
reme qualities, if you find such a man or men, consider them to be most
assuredly of high merit. You should indeed do so because they had the will
to be of high merit, and indeed they have been and are of high merit, and
they strive to their utmost to be of high merit until death. And it is good to
take such men as examples and to strive to act in such a way as to resemble   25
them. You should know that in no way can anyone in the world, now or in
the past or the future, ever have such a complete set of good qualifications
as have been described above as possessed by men of high merit, except
purely by the grace of God and of His gentle Mother and of His heavenly
court. And thus it is that these people whom Our Lord has of His grace   30
endowed with so many gifts should not maintain nor think nor believe
that in any way do any of these virtues listed above, for which they are so
much loved, praised and honored, come from themselves. Indeed no, for if
they had such an overweaningly proud thought, just as certainly as snow
melts away through the powerful heat directed on it by the sun, so would   35
it be for all the good things, the favors, the honors, the high estate, the
power, the beauty, the intelligence, the worth, the prowess, and the other
strengths which might be found in some one. Were these men to claim the
credit for all these qualities, believing that they all stem from themselves,
and were they not to give thanks as they should and it is their duty to do   40
to this mighty sun, to this Almighty Lord from whom they have received
them and hold them and do not acknowledge this, then this Almighty
Lord would cause all these benefits, so ill merited and unacknowledged, to
crumble and collapse in various ways, as, for example, by chronic illness
through which they would lose the glory they had won. Thus many of the   45
benefits, the favors, and the honors which in such a short time are forgotten
and lapse into oblivion, and the high position and power are soon reduced
to nothing by the force of their enemies, which increases so that they are

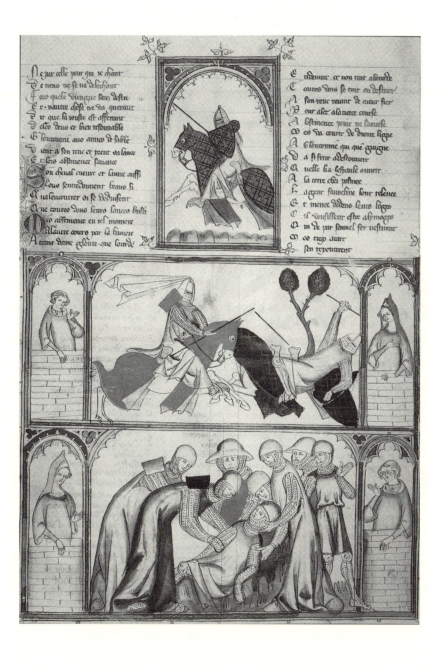

Ne pur celle pour qui ie chant
De nens ne se ua deseschant
Eco quele bienzie sans destr...
Er nautre chose ne va querant
Er que sa touste est affermnt
Euo deus et bien resonmable
Et leuronnue auo armes desable
Vient a son rene et prent en lance
Et leto abstinence suiuane
Son cheual cueur et lautre auffi
Sous sentredonnent brano fi
A salencontrer si se adduifent
Que toutes deus seurs sances bris...
Deo abstinence en tel momene
Dellautre cours par sa sumere
Aceste dame gefdite que lourde

En demur et vou tint afcourde
Toutes sois se tint ou destrier
A son rene reuint de cuer fier
Pour aser a latierce course
Abstinence point ne siourse
Eo ssu cours de droite siegne
A eteuronme qui que ezuigne
A si feeur addestouuer
Duelle sia lespaule ornent
La tene chu pstnee
Lacquir samestine sont reseue
Er mene dedens seurs soges
Er il consistent este afsimogeos
An de pur samel ser uestient
Eo trop atart
sen repenterent

brought down from this high position and their power is greatly diminished. As for beauty, it soon fades and vanishes, and because of this Our   50
Lord grants beauty to the unworthy so that the worthy may not attach too
great importance to it. As for intelligence, you can be certain that when
Our Lord wants to harm the wise who do not acknowledge Him, He takes
away their intelligence, as One who has the power to take away just as He
has the power to give. And as for the reputation for worth on account of   55
which some might have the foolish belief that they were not and could not
be guilty of sin, it is this very belief which makes them fail in their intention,
for they should not attribute this grace to themselves but to Almighty God
who gives such gifts; it is He to whom thanks should be given and to whom
entreaties should be made. And if these men do otherwise, they fall under   60
the dominion and power of the devil who will lead them into sin and damnation. And as for the skills and achievements of prowess which are acquired through great effort and danger over a number of years, in one hour
they can be and have been lost for lack of gratitude towards Him who
granted them. But nowadays shame is so familiar and honor so unfamiliar   65
that little account is taken of them, but those who put great effort into
acquiring these honorable skills and achievements of prowess and those to
whom God has by His grace granted that they should acquire them should
indeed spend all their time giving thanks, praising and honoring Our Lord,
praying and entreating humbly that as He has given and granted to them,   70
so He will not take away and withdraw according to what they deserve.
And so that you may have sure and certain knowledge of the things said
above, that is, that no one should be confident concerning any good within
him, that it can be put to any good use unless it be acknowledged that it
comes from the Lord and depends upon Him, you can take Samson as a   75
true example from ancient times: he was so strong, as the old accounts tell
us, that through despair and through hatred he tore down the pillar of a
building to kill himself and all the others who were inside, and through this
he greatly misused his strength. And there was Absalom, who was as handsome as anyone could be and had the most beautiful hair in the world;   80
through the delight he took in his beauty, as he rode beneath a tree, his hair
became entangled in that tree and he remained hanging by his beautiful
hair and died there. And there was Solomon, who was so very wise; as it
is told in the ancient accounts, he made such ill use of his intelligence, that
because of his wife's admonitions he began to adore idols, and in this way   85
seemed to abandon the worship of God; he therefore failed most shamefully in relation to his wisdom. And when one speaks of great worthiness,

St. Peter, who steadfastly loved and believed in Our Lord as His true disciple and apostle, did he not deny him thrice in one night with words from his lips but not from his heart; on each of these three occasions, he committed mortal sin, for which he soon repented, by the grace of Our Lord, as His true disciple; nevertheless he sinned. Therefore it would be a great thing for men of worth, if they could be as steadfast in the faith of Our Lord as was this holy man of worth, St. Peter, who lived in such a holy way and who is so honored for his saintly life. And as for military achievement, there was Julius Caesar, who was such a very good knight and engaged in so many great and wonderful battles and made so many fine conquests for those of Rome. On his return from all his glorious battles and all his fine and rich conquests, when he came back to Rome, he saw and understood that through envy the people of Rome did not show him as much honor as they were wont to do to other men who had conquered and fought for the honor and profit of Rome and who had not done as much as he had, so it seemed to him. Then his heart was filled with great anger and hatred against the people of Rome, the city from which he himself came, so much so that after that he waged war on them and inflicted great losses and overcame them and had himself crowned emperor of Rome. He gave them strong government and forbade the bearing of any knife or sword in his Senate House for fear lest they might kill him, for he could not trust them. What happened then was that the evil men who so hated and envied him had the idea of carrying styles with their tablets, apparently for writing, and by this means they were to kill him. When the emperor went into the Senate House, one of those who knew about this wicked enterprise wanted to warn him of this and gave him, as he walked alone, a letter in which this plot was set out; but he did not read it, rather he carried it away in his hand, from which great harm came to him. When he entered the Senate House and the doors were shut, then the wicked traitors took their styles and with these stabbed him to death very painfully and cruelly, and this was a grievous loss of such a good knight, so worthy and so valiant. But no one should become so annoyed and full of such ill will if he is not given the honor he should receive for such feats of arms, especially not against his lord or his own men; nor ought one to want to harm nor show hatred as Caesar did to the men of Rome, for which he himself died so strangely and painfully as has been told above. And perhaps, if he had not turned against the men of Rome, he might have lived longer and with great honor among all kinds of people as the very perfect knight that he was. Therefore no one should have too high an opinion of himself nor should he expect too much praise nor place too much value on it, for the good things and honors of this world are not certain and constant except insofar as it may please God who grants these benefits and from whom they are held. And those who perform great deeds should know that no great deed can be lost or hidden so that it is unknown and forgotten, but such deeds should be talked of and made known by the friends and enemies of those who perform them and many other people besides. And those who have performed these great deeds should not be concerned with this but only with thanking God, that Lord by whose grace these deeds can be achieved, in such a way that He should regard with favor those to whom He has granted these achievements for the true acknowledgment and service they give Him in return; nothing else should matter to them provided they continue to perform great deeds. And may he who wishes say it, and he who wishes remain silent about it: the men of worth are always those who get furthest. Now each of you can know and be certain that there is no wisdom, worthiness, strength, beauty, prowess, or valor that may be found in anyone and may remain and endure save only by the grace of Our Lord. And some might say that all these above-mentioned graces and virtues cannot be found in one man alone, and they might well be speaking the truth according to the time and the circumstances to be found today; yet all those who were willing to devote themselves entirely to winning these high honors, which they must achieve by force of arms and by heroic deeds, should be intent on learning how the best knights there ever were came by and won the noble qualities and high honors of which there is so much and so truly said, as the Bible testifies. And as it would take too long to recall all these knights, a brief and true account could be given of the excellent knight Judas Maccabeus, of whom it can be said that in him alone were to be found all the good qualities set out above. He was wise in all his deeds, he was a man of worth who led a holy life, he was strong, skillful, and unrelenting in effort and endurance; he was handsome above all others, and without arrogance; he was full of prowess, bold, valiant, and a great fighter, taking part in the finest, greatest, and fiercest battles and the most perilous adventures there ever were, and in the end he died in a holy way in battle, like a saint in paradise. And this is true, for in all his deeds and throughout his life this good knight conducted himself according to the true belief, trust, and hope in Our Lord, thanking Him devoutly for all the benefits and honors which came to him. And Our Lord, for the great faith that this good knight had in Him and the understanding he had of Him, comforted, guided, and helped him in all his great, noble, and honorable deeds; and the Bible, in which lies the truth,

130

135

140

145

150

155

160

165

bears witness that all his actions were without pride, envy, or greed, and directed only toward performing great deeds and defeating his enemies in order to uphold and maintain belief in God. For all this it was the will of Our Lord that he should be accepted into His glorious company and num- bered among the saints and that the memory of his great chivalry should 170 be celebrated for ever. Ah God! what a splendid example is this for all knights and all men-at-arms who aim to attain these heights of prowess and valor whereby so many good deeds are performed and win recognition dur- ing the lifetime of such men and for so long after their death. And in rela- tion to those who might reflect on and consider the life devoted to good 175 and to great deeds of this fine and saintly knight described above, whom one would like to resemble as closely as possible in his good way of life, it could be maintained confidently and firmly that such people who would thus desire to conduct their way of life and behavior could not and should not fail to attain the high honor of chivalry, in terms of both soul and body. 180 There are indeed many, who can achieve much renown for physical achieve- ment, whose souls are afterward lost; and there are others who have won little renown for these high honors while their souls have gone to their salvation in the company of Our Lord; but the man to whom God by His grace grants high honor in this world and in the end the soul's acceptance 185 in paradise, as He did to this excellent above-mentioned knight and to a number of others, such a man could not ask for more from God. Were anyone, therefore, to say that those who are engaged in a career of arms would not be able to save their souls, they would not know what they were saying, for in all good, necessary, and traditional professions anyone can 190 lose or save his soul as he wills. But when in the profession of arms, in which one can and should win these high honors, one can indeed make one's personal career honorably and valiantly and save one's soul, as for example in the practice of arms in wars which have been begun in the proper manner and in due form and in the battles which ensue. This is 195 the case when lords have wars, and their men can and should fight for them and move confidently and bravely into battle for such causes, for if one performs well there, one is honored in life, and if one dies there, one's soul is saved, if other sins do not stand in the way of this. In addition, if someone is intent on disinheriting a man's kinsman or if there is a need to defend 200 their estate, when under such compulsion, men can embark on wars and battles without fear for body and soul, for the circumstances make this le- gitimate and of necessity. And again, if some people wanted to seize the land and inheritance of defenseless maidens or widows and could not be

dissuaded from this except by war or combat, one ought to embark on this   205
confidently in regard to one's personal reputation and the saving of one's
soul, and the same is true in relation to the defense of orphans. And for
even better reason, one can wage war and embark on battles on one's own
account to defend one's land and inheritance when it cannot be defended
in any other way, and this can be done without endangering one's personal   210
honor or soul. And again, to preserve and maintain the rights of the Holy
Church, one should not hold back from committing oneself to their defense by war and battle, if they cannot be maintained in any other way. And
the man who acts thus wins in noble fashion personal honor and the salvation of his soul. Moreover, the man who makes war against the enemies of   215
religion in order to support and maintain Christianity and the worship
of Our Lord is engaged in a war which is righteous, holy, certain, and sure,
for his earthly body will be honored in a saintly fashion and his soul will, in
a short space of time, be borne in holiness and without pain into paradise.
This kind of war is good, for one can lose in it neither one's reputation in   220
this world nor one's soul. Nor ought one to fear those wars mentioned
above which are started from great necessity and to protect one's rights,
provided they are carried on and conducted in such a way that one is always
in such a state of purity of conscience that one does not and should not fear
to die in order to avoid all shame, which in this pursuit of arms can often   225
happen to those whom God does not graciously protect from such things.
And because of this each person ought to be aware and bear in mind that
in all the callings there are in the world, whether religious or secular, in
which anyone should or might be engaged, no men have so great a need
for a clear conscience as is required of men-at-arms. It can indeed be shown   230
that this is so, for if anyone will reflect and consider how the order of chivalry was founded and established and how it should be entered devoutly
and in a holy manner, one might say that this order, when it is well conducted for the purpose and in the manner that the order of chivalry should
be conducted, might of all orders be the supreme order, except for the di-   235
vine service. For you should know that the other orders, that is the religious
orders, were and still are established and ordained to serve God and to pray
to Him on behalf of themselves and of others, whether living or dead, and
to take no account of nor delight in worldly things; and they can and indeed
ought to conduct themselves in this way, when their manner and place of   240
living is ordained and laid down: to dwell in abbeys and in cloisters, in the
places ordained for the service of Our Lord and for such prayers, orisons,
and fastings that they are bound and obliged to perform by their vows, each

one according to the articles of their religious rules; they are spared the
physical danger and the strenuous effort of going out onto the field of battle   245
to take up arms, and are also spared the threat of death. Therefore they do
and should do that for which their way of life has been established and
ordained in such peaceful terms. But as for the order of chivalry, it can truly
be said and demonstrated that it is the most dangerous for both soul and
body, and the one in which it is necessary to maintain a clearer conscience   250
than in any other order in the world.

The Knighting Ceremony

36   And in order that it should be better understood why and for what
good reasons the rite of entry into the order of chivalry was established, it
is best to describe how it is performed and thus give a greater knowledge
of it. You should know that when a new knight is to be made, first of all he
must confess, repent of all his sins, and make sure that he is in a fit state to   5
receive the body of Our Lord [the Host]. On the eve of the ceremony, all
those who are to be knighted the next day should enter a bath and stay there
for a long time, reflecting on the need to cleanse their bodies henceforth
from all impurities of sin and dishonorable ways of life; they should leave
all such impurities in the water. Then they should come out of the water in   10
the bath with a clear conscience and should go and lie in a new bed in clean
white sheets; there they should rest as those who have emerged from a great
struggle against sin and from the great peril of the devils' torment. The bed
signifies repose, stemming from virtue, from a clear conscience, from making one's peace with God with regard to all past actions that might have   15
angered Him. Then the knights should come to the beds to dress those to
be knighted; the stuff in which they dress them, the linen and all that goes
with it should be new: this signifies that just as the body of each one should
be cleansed of all the impurities of sin, so should it be clothed in new, white,
and clean material, signifying that they should all from henceforth keep   20
themselves pure and free from sin. Then the knights should robe them in
red tunics, signifying that they are pledged to shed their blood to defend
and maintain the faith of Our Lord and the rights of the Holy Church and
all the other just rights set out above which it is the knight's duty to protect.
Then the knights bring black hose and put them on those to be knighted;   25
this signifies that they should remember that from the earth they have come
and to the earth they must return for the death which awaits them, they
know not at what hour; therefore they should put all pride beneath their
feet. Then the knights bring them white belts with which they gird them,

signifying that they should surround their bodies with chastity and purity   30
of the flesh. After that the knights bring them red cloaks and place them on
their shoulders as a sign of great humility, for cloaks in this form were made
in ancient times in all humility. Then the knights bring them joyfully into
the church, and in the church they must remain and keep vigil all night until
dawn, praying very devoutly to Our Lord that it may please Him to forgive   35
the unworthy sleeping and watching of which they have been guilty in the
past and that He grant them to keep vigil henceforth in His grace and in
His service. The next day, the knights bring them to mass, to hear it devoutly, praying to Our Lord that He may grant them grace to enter and
maintain this order in His service and His grace. When mass has been sung,   40
the knights lead them to the person or persons destined to confer the order.
For each one to be knighted he gives two gilded spurs, one to each of two
knights; these two knights each fasten one to a foot, signifying that gold is
the most coveted of all metals and is placed on their feet as a sign that they
should remove from their hearts all unworthy covetousness of riches. Then   45
the knight who is to confer the order of knighthood takes a sword; as the
sword cuts on both sides of the blade, so should they defend and maintain
right, reason, and justice on all sides without being false to the Christian
faith or to the rights of the Holy Church for anyone. Then the knights who
confer the order on them should kiss them as a sign of confirmation of the   50
order conferred on them and received by them, and that peace, love, and
loyalty may be in them; thus should they strive on behalf of and uphold the
order with all their hearts wherever they can. Then these knights should
give them the *collee* [a light tap, probably here with sword] as a sign that
they should for ever more remember this order of knighthood which they   55
have received and carry out all the activities that may pertain to this order.
And thus are these things done and so should they be done. Those are
blessed by fortune who conduct themselves in such a manner as the estate
requires. If anyone does the contrary, it would have been better for him
never to have been made a knight. It can be held that there are three differ-   60
ent ways of entering the order of knighthood. Some may choose to enter it
when young, so that they can strive longer without fear and without sparing their bodies or possessions in all the services and conditions which pertain, can and should pertain to knighthood. Others want to have the order
of knighthood so that people will say that they are knights and so that they   65
will receive greater attention and honor than they did before; but they do
not want to fulfill the true conditions and services of knighthood. For that
reason it might be said of these men that they may well have the order of

knighthood but not the reputation of being a knight, for men may have the
order who are not real knights. There are also some ancient men of worth   70
who want to spend their old age and end their days in the order of knighthood; they want to enter at this advanced age and they can indeed do so in
keeping with the estate of knighthood, for they should have more sense and
judgment than the young, and all the qualities of maturity and of virtuous
living ought to be in them. Thus they can give help and comfort in many   75
good and needful ways through their good sense, and the good young
knights can do their part with their swords, maintaining and protecting the
faith, reason, and justice. Good knights can and should live loyally and
honorably.

The Order of Marriage

37   Having considered the order of knighthood, it is appropriate to turn
our attention to the order of marriage. There are three possible ways of
entering into marriage. Some men and women marry when the man has
no carnal knowledge of a woman, nor a woman of a man, and they do it
more for love than for greed for riches; such a marriage is good in that   5
it provides heirs and saves the man and woman from sin. There are some
who pay no regard to the person when entering into marriage, but do so
out of greed for riches; in the case of those who marry more for gain than
for any other pleasure, it is unlikely that any good will come of it, for indeed the devils must be at their wedding. Then there are some who are   10
widowers, have children, are old, and marry more to keep themselves from
sin than to have descendants, nor could they because of their age; these
can live fittingly within the order of marriage. It is those who conduct
themselves most properly in the order of marriage who live joyfully and
pleasantly.   15

The Monastic Orders

38   Then one can consider the holy monastic orders, which can be entered
in three different ways. First, when one enters so young that one has no
knowledge of sin nor of the world; those who enter at such an age are
brought up in the order and should accept it more willingly; they should,
therefore, conduct themselves better and adhere more closely to the rules   5
of the religious order. There might also be some who, after having for a
long time lived in and known the world and after having committed dishonorable deeds often and over a lengthy period, want to enter a religous
order, lightly and without being truly devout. Then it is very hard for them

to keep to and follow the right paths and the precepts and rules to which   10
religious are required to adhere, and they are very reluctant to do so. It has
all too often been seen that as far as a number of such people are concerned,
it would have been better for the religious orders if they had never entered
them, as shame is brought to the monastic orders and to the good religious
by the disordered and dishonorable lives led by such unruly brothers. Such   15
men belong to the order but are not religious. Then there are some who
have reached old age and are no longer capable of striving in this world,
and they leave it to enter religious orders so that they can end their days in
a more salutary way, for both their bodies and their souls; and this is right.
Therefore good religious can and should live in an orderly and holy way. It   20
is, therefore, possible and right to maintain that for the three orders considered above it can and should be most fitting and best to enter a religious
order when young, marriage when young, and arms and knighthood when
young.

The Order of Priesthood

39   We could also speak briefly of the worthiest order of all, that of priesthood. In this order, unlike those considered above in relation to entry when
young, no one should enter it unless he learns as a youth his service, which
he must study and know very well; for there are many who begin so young
that they know nothing of it and have no understanding of it, and this can   5
give rise to great dangers. There are also many who do have an understanding of it, but they do not conduct themselves as befits their office; it ill
behooves them not to behave properly, in accordance with the worthy office which they have entered upon and which they have undertaken. But
there are those who have set their minds to it and know and perform their   10
service well and sing and chant devoutly and know how to behave in a
manner befitting the noble estate of an ordained priest. Such priests can do
much good in three ways by their devout prayers to that very high Lord
whom they so often hold in their hands: first, they can pray for themselves,
second, for the souls of the departed, third, for those who are still living   15
whom they remember. These good priests can and should live righteous
and devout lives. It is also true that in the order of marriage, where it is well
conducted as is befitting and should befit the said order, one can and should
live at ease in heart, body, and soul. And as for the holy religious orders,
the good brothers know the hours when they should serve Our Lord by   20
going into church, they know the hours when they should eat, drink, sleep,
and care little for the world. These good secular priests who have such a

noble office to perform should and can live at peace in heart and good conscience. It is not for them to undertake other duties, and if they behave in
this way, they act in keeping with their position and as befits their office.   25
They should not have anything to do except say their masses with diligence
and devotion, and this office should suffice without learning any other.

The Rigors of the Order of Knighthood

40   After speaking of all these orders, it is now time to return to the good
order of knighthood, which should be considered the most rigorous order
of all, especially for those who uphold it well and conduct themselves in a
manner in keeping with the purpose for which the order was established. It
will indeed be apparent that, however much it may be said to those entering   5
the religious orders that when they want to eat, they will fast, and when
they want to fast, then they will have to eat, when they want to sleep, they
will have to keep vigil, and many other such things, this is all nothing in
comparison with the suffering to be endured in the order of knighthood.
For, whoever might want to consider the hardships, pains, discomforts,   10
fears, perils, broken bones, and wounds which the good knights who uphold the order of knighthood as they should endure and have to suffer frequently, there is no religious order in which as much is suffered as has to
be endured by these good knights who go in search of deeds of arms in
the right way as has been set forth above. No one can and should excuse   15
himself from bearing arms in a just cause, whether for his lord or for his
lineage or for himself or for the Holy Church or to defend and uphold the
faith or out of pity for men or women who cannot defend their own rights.
In such cases they should commit themselves eagerly, boldly, and gladly to
such deeds of arms and adventures, fearing nothing. Hence it should be   20
understood that good knights may have to undergo hard trials and adventures, for it can truly be said to them that when they want to sleep, they
must keep vigil, when they want to eat, they must fast, and when they are
thirsty, there is often nothing to drink, and when they would rest, they have
to exert themselves all through the night, and when they would be secure   25
from danger, they will be beset by great terrors, and when they would defeat their enemies, sometimes they may be defeated or killed or captured
and wounded and struggling to recover; this is not to speak of the perilous
adventures they may encounter on their journeys in search of deeds of arms,
such as the danger of crossing sea or river, of passing over treacherous   30
places or bridges, of encountering riots or robbers. All these dangers must
they endure and come through safely when they can and God grants them

grace. And where are the orders which could suffer as much? Indeed, in this order of knighthood, one can well save the soul and bring honor to the body. [Nevertheless those who perform deeds of arms more for glory in   35 this world] than for the salvation of the soul, may sometimes gain honor and renown, but the souls will profit little, and the renown will be the briefer for it. And for those who perform deeds of arms more to gain God's grace and for the salvation of the soul than for glory in this world, their noble souls will be set in paradise to all eternity and their persons will be   40 for ever honored and well remembered. Thus it is for all those who go in search of deeds of arms in support of the right, whether or not they be knights, for many fine men-at-arms are as good as knights, and this is true also of some seculars as it is of some good religious.

Those Unworthy To Be Men-at-Arms

41   And as for those men who take up arms, but are not men-at-arms, nor is it right that they should be because of their very dishonest and disordered behavior under these arms, it is these men who want to wage war without good reason, who seize other people without prior warning and with-out any good cause and rob and steal from them, wound and kill them.   5 Those who use arms in this dishonorable way behave like cowards and traitors, nor would they dare to bear arms in any other way. They attack anyone, taking booty, prisoners, and other valuables, if they find them, and without any justification. There are some who want people to believe that they themselves would never commit such wicked deeds, but they have   10 them done by their own men. There are others who say that they them-selves would never engage in such evil works, but they receive those who commit such ill deeds and support them and like them and value them the better for it. Hence it is often said that he does mischief enough who helps mischief. Indeed all such people who are thus doers or consenters or   15 receivers in relation to such deeds are not worthy to live or to be in the company of men of worth; for they have no regard for themselves: how could they hold others in regard? They have no desire to live a valiant and good life: how could they advise others to do so? They do not care whether people speak well of them: how could they speak well of others? They have   20 no desire to perform deeds which will bring them worthy benefits: how could they achieve this for others? They are not willing to act in a way which will bring them honor: how are they going to honor others? They lack all power of judgment: how could they behave reasonably to others? It could be said that such wicked men who practice arms in so many evil ways are   25

characterized by four very bad forms of ill doing. The first is that of robbery on the highway, treacherously stealing and for no good reason. The second is to murder others in a bad cause. The third is to commit a treacherous deed by seizing, plundering, and robbing others without any challenge and without any wrongdoing on the part of the persons attacked. And the 30 fourth is to take from the churches the wealth through which Our Lord is served and to harm those persons who are ordained to perform such a noble office as to serve God, and by such evil deeds this noble service will not be carried out. Thus they could be held to be nothing more than bad Christians. And cursed be these persons who devote their lives to commit- 35 ting such evil deeds in order to acquire such dishonorable ill fame! And indeed any lords who have such men under their control and have knowl- edge of their ill doings are no longer worthy to live if they do not inflict such punishment on them that would persuade anyone else who might have a desire for wrongdoing to draw back. And is it not greatly to be 40 wondered at that such people should subject themselves to the great physi- cal trials of enduring great hardships and exertions throughout night, of riding night and day, of sleeping little and having poor food and drink, of being often in fear and peril, at the mercy of all kinds of hazards, all this, only to lose their lives and their honor and to damn their souls for ever? It 45 means great penance for them in this world and even greater in the next for all eternity.

The Orders of Priesthood and Knighthood Compared

42 It is right that after treating such wretched subject matter we should resume our discussion of good knights and good men-at-arms who do not and would not take up arms for any unworthy undertaking nor in order to commit base deeds but only to perform deeds that are good, just and hon- orable, free from all reproach. It is certain that it can and should be fitting 5 that all these good men-at-arms don their armor in as pure and devout a way and with as good a conscience as should priests don the armor of Our Lord to sing the mass and conduct the divine service. And in order to have a better understanding of this, you should know that it behooves all priests who are ordained for such a high service to lead honest lives; and when 10 they come into the church to sing the mass, they ought to come there cleansed from all their sins and very devout, and in a pure and holy state of mind should take up the arms of Our Lord against the devils of hell lest these prevent them from fulfillling their duty in this noble service for which Our Lord has given them the power to consecrate His own body in their 15 hands, which is then shown to us by them through God's grace every day in the Holy Church. Such men, who are ordained to perform this holy service, should lead pure and saintly lives. And they can and ought to do so in holiness and in security, for if they have the will to have a clear conscience and to be free from sin, they need fear nothing, for as long as they are in that state, they have no need to be afraid of devils, who are the most powerful enemies they have to deal with, for they should not have to fear enemies of this world, nor should they deserve to have any enemies, nor would one expect any men to be hostile to them or harm them. And they can perform their office in security, for in that situation God is with them visibly. In holding this glorious service in the churches, where they perform it, they are secure. And all those who come there should come devoutly and obediently to hear and see the service and to obey the holy commandments of our faith and to remember them and to act according to them, and to honor those by whom such services are performed and such great and good truth announced. Now you can see that such good priests have the opportunity, if they avail themselves of it, to take up the arms of Our Lord to perform this glorious service in a holy way, in security and without fear if they do not hesitate. But of the good knights and good men-at-arms who, in pursuit of all the benefits mentioned earlier, desire often to take up arms, it might well be considered that they should be of as great or even greater integrity than might be required of a priest, for they are in danger every day, and at the moment when they think themselves to be the most secure, it is then that they may suddenly have to take up arms and often to undertake demanding and dangerous adventures. And is it not essential for such good men-at-arms that when they want to take up and don their armor, which can and should be called the armor of Our Lord, when donned to defend right and justice, that they should put it on in true and pure devoutness, having confessed all their sins and repented of them, praying to Our Lord that He forgive their misdeeds and that it may please Him to come to their aid? And it behooves them to seek in humble devotion for the help of Our Lord in such a perilous service as is required of them in the vocation of arms, for this service may not fittingly be performed in churches, which are beautiful and strong, nor can it by its nature be carried out there nor in safe places, but such services must perforce be performed on the field and in such danger as can and should pertain to such a calling and to the performance of the service for which such men take up arms. And those who come to encounter the men who perform such service do not come to honor those who are the leaders in such a service, but they

come there to kill, disinherit, or dishonor them, if they can, and to take 55
everything from them if they have the power. And through this one can
know and fully understand that such a service and calling, which can well
be performed according to God's will, is very dangerous and perilous, and
its practice makes greater physical and spiritual demands than those required of any of the men who are ordained to serve Our Lord in the Holy 60
Church, for they have and ought to have their rule and ordinance and position for the conduct of both their lives and the service it is their duty to
perform; but these good men-at-arms have no rule or ordinance to observe
in relation to their their way of life and their position except to love and
fear God always and to take care not to anger Him, and to be themselves 65
always in such a situation that they are all the time more engaged in such
dangerous enterprises than any other men. Hence one could well say truly
that of all the men in the world, of whatever estate, whether religious or
lay, none have as great a need to be a good Christian to the highest degree
nor to have such true devoutness in their hearts nor to lead a life of such 70
integrity and to carry out all their undertakings loyally and with good
judgment as do these good men-at-arms who have the will to pursue this
calling, as has been set out above, wisely and according to God's will. For
there is in such men no firm purpose to cling to life; they should rather
show firmness in the face of death and be prepared to meet it at any time, 75
for it often happens that these people die without the leisure to fall ill
of fever or other physical ailments from which a person might suffer for
a long time and reflect on his past deeds. Indeed, let anyone consider
all these perilous adventures which may in a brief span be encountered by
these men-at-arms who choose to make the appropriate personal and physi- 80
cal effort to achieve the high reputation for valor which is of such great
worth and is in accord with the will of God. It is indeed so prized, praised,
and honored that one can say in all certainty that of all the conditions of
this world, it is the one above all others in which one would be required to
live with the constant thought of facing death at any hour on any day; for 85
of all conditions it is the one in which one's life is least secure, for it is a life
spent in great effort and endurance and perilous adventure arising from
others' hate and envy, where many would like to cause one's death. Therefore the position and way of life of these men-at-arms should above all be
devoted to serving with all their hearts Our Lord and the glorious Virgin 90
Mary in return for the good comfort and honorable escape from death
which Our Lord has granted them from day to day. And indeed, if they did
not act in this way, all their undertakings would come to a miserable end,

and examples of this are often to be seen, such as losing one's honor or one's life or one's fortune, and sometimes all of them together and one's soul as 95 well, through lack of gratitude to Our Lord for the gifts He has bestowed on many who do not give Him thanks for them and repent too late of this, for there might be no time left. And is it not right that if some one receives a gift from another, he should be required to give something in return? And it has often been seen to happen that men of the most evil way of life, of 100 whom there are many to be found in this world, refrain from harming those from whom they have received some benefits, like thieves and robbers, who often stop stealing from those who have in some way done them favors, and like some murderers, who kill people to get their possessions and in the same way hold back from murdering those from whom they have received 105 some favors, and like some traitors, who have chosen not to betray or have given information to those from whom they have received some benefit. These people of such bad character and who are so intent on evil doing, in this evil doing want to give something in return for those benefits they have received from others by not practicing their evil doing on them. Is there 110 not, therefore, even greater reason that those who have no intention of committing such misdeeds or leading such wicked lives, ought to give more in return for the benefits, profits, honors, or services they have received from another, and in many better ways than should those above-mentioned evil men? Indeed yes. And where could one find anyone who can and does 115 always bestow so many benefits, favors, mercies, honors, and every kind of perfection and good other than that very glorious Lord who is up above and His glorious Virgin Mother? They give to all those who ask in the right way and with such devoutness as is fitting for requests made to such a Lord and such a Lady, who have bestowed so great an abundance of 120 benefits on those who have the will to serve them with all their hearts and to give something in return for these benefits to those who grant them. It is indeed the Sovereign Lord in whom all that is good is to be found and from whom all that is good comes and for whom all good is done and who has the power to give all good things, whenever it is His will, 125 and to make them last as long as it pleases Him, and who also has the power to take them away, whenever it pleases Him, from those who do not ac-knowledge Him. Therefore no one should consider that the good done them by others, or honors bestowed on them by others, or service done them by others, or any profit deriving from others, that any of these come only 130 from other people. These benefits come rather from the grace of God whom it pleases that these things should be done, for it should be known that no one has anything in the world which is certainly his except in so far as it pleases God who lends everything and can take back everything as the true Sovereign Lord that He is, with everything dependent on His will. 135 And when it is the duty of these men to acknowledge and they are required to serve those from whom they receive some benefit, they ought then indeed to serve and acknowledge, praise and be in awe of, honor and worship a hundredfold and infinitely more with all their hearts, totally, humbly, and devoutly this glorious Lord and His glorious Virgin Mother, For those 140 who pass on to others these benefits and favors have themselves been granted them by God as a loan and dependent on His will: they have nothing of these favors and benefits except what God allows them and lends them of His grace, and they have nothing more. But there are many who pay little heed to the source of these benefits, favors, honors, high positions, 145 and lordships which come to them, but grab them in such an unseemly fashion as is to be seen today; and when Our Lord by His will allows some to have benefits and honors from which they gain some kind of renown, it seems to them that this renown should last for ever without coming to an end, and that it should always happen to them like this. And if in the past 150 they happen to have achieved something which increased their good name, some reflect on how they might make it last, and they no longer remember Our Lord and begin to think only of the pleasures of this world, and they present themselves in their ways of behavior and bearing as better than they either are or are held to be by others. And if they have any financial 155 resources, they cannot bring themselves to devote a fourth part to honoring Our Lord or His gentle Mother or the Saints or the Holy Church, or to giving alms to the poor or paying what they owe or settling their debts to others, for they want to spend it all on adorning their wretched bodies and on decking themselves out with precious stones, pearls, fine work, and em- 160 broidery, which cost so much and are worth so little, and on buying the rings on their fingers and great bands of gold and silver of which the workmanship costs many times more than the gold or silver of which they are made. And it would be better for them now to put this expenditure to better use, for which Our Lord would look more favorably upon them and 165 would give them so much in return that they could not ask for a greater or better reward. But just as they forget God for the sake of such paltry trifles, so God too will forget them. And because of this they will no longer win the great benefits and honors they won at the outset, for they deck out with rich adornments their wretched bodies, destined to endure for so short a time, and all that is left to contemplate in these men is that which at any time may vanish away, even while they think everyone should hold them to be of great account. And they are dressed in such an indecent way that that which everyone ought to be most ashamed to show is what they show all the time to those who want to look, for they cannot refrain from showing their backsides to whoever wants to see them. And if they want to sit down, they do not have enough to cover themselves neither in front nor behind, and they feel no shame about showing what should cause them such great shame. And it is to be expected that the excessive adornments with which they deck themselves out make them neglect to perform many great deeds; and there are many who forget all shame, and just as they forget all shame, so is all honor forgotten; this can be seen in various forms of behavior, which is a great pity. What is more, it is not enough for them to be as God made them; they are not content with themselves as they are, but they gird themselves up and so rein themselves in round the middle of their bodies that they seek to deny the existence of the stomachs which God has given them: they want to pretend that they have not and never have had one, and everyone knows that the opposite is true. And one has seen many of those thus constricted who have to take off their armor in a great hurry, for they could no longer bear to wear their equipment; and there are others who have been quickly seized, for they could not do what they should have done because they were handicapped by being thus constricted; and many have died inside their armor for the same reason, that they could put up little defense. And even without their armor they are so constricted and strapped up that they cannot undertake anything, for they cannot bend down, nor can they run nor jump nor throw stones nor engage in any other sports requiring strength or agility; indeed they can hardly sit down, and it demands just as great an effort to struggle to their feet again. There might be some who would prefer to give the appearance of being a good man-at-arms rather than the reality, but no one, however devious or simple, would doubt that when it comes to achieving something, whether in or out of armor, it is those who perform the greatest deeds whose names are on everyone's lips and who are most honored. It is God's will that it should be so, for Our Lord bestows his benefits where he sees they will be best used, and from Him come also the disgrace and ill fortune which he bestows on those who think they can have the benefits and honors by their own efforts without remembering Him; and this should be accepted as the truth. But

there is no reason why it should not and cannot be fitting for young men in all circumstances, whether at home or on the field, to be dressed decently, neatly, elegantly, with due restraint and with attractive things of low cost   210
and often replaced; for it is right that people should behave, each according to their years, provided so much be not devoted to adornment of the body that the more important things remain undone, that is to say, great and good deeds. And if anyone is thus elegantly dressed and in good fashion, as befits a young man, it should not be done through pride nor should Our   215
Lord be forgotten; but be careful not to spruce yourself up so much that you do not remember God, for if you do not remember God, God will not remember you. But one should dress well when in company with other young people and to fit in with them; and it is a fine and good thing to spend one's youth in honest fashion, and those who spend it thus should   220
praise God all their lives.

What Young Ladies Should Wear

43   As for the youth of noble ladies, damsels, and other women of high rank, it can indeed be said that for those of them who are in a position to do so, it is fitting to wear fine circlets, coronetals, pearls, precious stones, rings, embroidery, to be beautifully dressed, their heads and bodies well adorned according to what is right and fitting for each person to do; it is   5
much more suitable for them to wear fine adornments than for men, for young damsels sometimes achieve better marriages when they are seen in rich apparel which suits them. And those who are married ought to maintain as high a standard of dress as they can, the better to please their husbands and to appear in appropriate fashion among other noble ladies and   10
damsels. And it behooves women of high rank to present themselves in the most stately apparel, wearing the richest adornments, and it befits them better than it does men, for the qualities and reputation of men are more quickly known and recognized and in more ways than the qualities and reputation of women can be known, for men go where they want among   15
people and in different lands, but women cannot do this. Men can joust and tourney: women cannot do this. Men take up arms for war: women cannot do this. Men go out more widely in society than women can. It is appropriate for women, because they spend more time at home than do men and do not often leave it and cannot get the same recognition, that   20
they should pay more attention to their physical appearance and be more splendidly adorned with jewels, rich ornaments, and apparel than would be suitable for men, who can in so many different ways win recognition

for their achievements. One should leave to noble ladies and damsels these rich adornments, the wearing of which suits them so much better than it does men, for by the goodness and beauty and fine behavior to be found in them, together with such adornments as are mentioned above, which suit them well, they receive recognition. These rich ornaments should be left to them. Therefore, for those who have the will to rise to great achievement, how can they better adorn themselves than by being equipped for it by all the good qualities? They can do so by being men of worth, wise, loyal, without arrogance, joyful, generous, courteous, expert, bold, and active, and of good conduct toward all others, without indulging in self praise or speaking ill of others. And if you want to wear such a garment as this, embroidered and richly worked with the qualities described above, and encrusted and decorated with those kinds of jewels, and to add to these the other qualities and precepts set out earlier, it could well be said that there is no garment, however short or tight, nor however well adorned with bands, precious stones, pearls, gold and silver straps, and all the other jewels, that could provide so great a protection against doing wrong, nor by which one could be better dressed, adorned, bejeweled, praised, loved, esteemed, and honored in the sight of God and all the world, as one would be through being invested and adorned with all those good qualities set out above. And those who have the greater amount of these qualities will be the more greatly praised and loved. And if you want to be armed elegantly and stylishly and desire that your arms be remembered, recognized, and adorned above others, seek constantly and diligently opportunities to perform deeds of arms. And when God grants you the good fortune to find them, do your duty wisely and boldly, fearing nothing except shame, striving with the skill of your hand and the effort of your body to as great a degree as your powers can extend in order to inflict damage on your opponents, always being among the first in battle. By so doing you will receive greater recognition for your achievements from your friends and enemies, and your arms will be splendid to behold, and you will through this appear more elegant and stylish under arms than you would if your equipment were strewn with pearls and precious stones, nor is there any embroidery which can be compared to this beauty. You should make your armor more elegant with such work; and whoever achieves the most is the most transformed and adorned. And if you want to be strong and securely armed against all the perils of the soul and against shame, and on many occasions against physical dangers, be careful to lead a life that will be pleasing to Our Lord, that He might have reason to remember you when you call upon Him in your times of great need, when in physical danger. And do not take up arms nor in any way put your life in danger without first seeking to be in such a good state in relation to God that He will listen to any entreaties and requests that you might with reason make to Him in your prayers, so that you should not fear death too much. And if you want to continue to achieve great deeds, exert yourself, take up arms, fight as you should, go everywhere across both land and sea and through many different countries, without fearing any peril and without sparing your wretched body, which you should hold to be of little account, caring only for your soul and for living an honorable life. If you do this, you will be everywhere safeguarded, loved, esteemed, and honored, recognized and remembered for your fine achievements and efforts and great feats among your friends and enemies and throughout many lands and marches, and even by those who never saw you and never will see you, and long after your death. Because of all this people will pray for you both during your lifetime and after your death, and your heirs and descendants will be honored afterward.

A Good Man-at-Arms Can Be Pleasing to God

44 Now one can see and know what a noble treasure it is to amass and gather together all these above-mentioned good achievements; and he who amasses and gathers together the most is supremely rich, adorned, valued, loved, feared, and pleasing to God and to all people. And fine grace and great worth are to be found in those who can live in secular terms the kind of lives through which mortal men can with honor in this world lead their souls into paradise in the next and take their place in that glorious company which will continue for ever in bliss without end. Ah God! how do those who commit evil deeds have the heart to do so when they see and know those who perform great deeds and do so with such confidence and joy, so honorably and pleasantly, and without fear of anyone, and coming to a good end; and wrongdoing is so perilous, so grievous, so dishonorable, so disgraceful, so unsure, and leading to a bad end? And how can one say anything but ill of those who have the choice and who have the skill and strength to perform worthy deeds, when they give up doing those things which are so assuredly honorable in order to do bad deeds which are so perilous to carry out and so shameful? And if you want to know how you will be encouraged in performing and multiplying all these great deeds and in abandoning any desire to commit all these evil deeds, pray with all your hearts to the glorious Virgin Mary that with her benign and humble grace   20 and by the holy influence she has over her precious, glorious and sovereign Lord, Father and Son, that of His noble gentle tender mercy He may, in his glory, look upon your hearts, bodies, and actions, and upon your souls, that He may preserve you, maintain and sustain you in a good state within His holy, benign grace, this grace which you should desire above all else   25 and with all your hearts to participate in from your beginnings until your ends. Now he is indeed a poor wretch who leaves this sweet spring at which everyone can quench his thirst and satisfy all his good desires, for he can only find there a good beginning, a better middle and a very good end. And this spring and all its streams are accessible to all those who have done   30 worthy deeds and want to partake of it. And if you want to drink from this spring, to be washed and purified by its streams, and to attain and fulfill all your good desires, remember the true source from which this spring comes: that is, to speak plainly, God our Creator, who chose to become incarnate by passing through this glorious spring of purity and virginity, the gentle   35 and glorious Virgin Mary. Therefore, from this glorious spring, so many streams spread out over us other poor sinners, as she prays for us and guides and teaches us, and brings us back by her gentle entreaties to the paths of righteousness and to a good end in relation to this glorious source, her dear and blessed Son. Now you who have the will to attain these great achieve-   40 ments and honors should not hesitate nor fear to subject your feeble bodies to danger, pain, and effort, of whatever rank you may be, each one accord- ing to his station in life, for there is no one, whether old or young, strong or weak, healthy or ill, rich or poor, who knows who is to die first. So one should lead a good life, and then one will be less afraid of death, and one   45 should indeed live at ease and fear nothing if one dwells in such good hope as one should have in the glorious Lord and His gentle and glorious Virgin Mother. And when one knows where one could find the foundation for all these good things which one should have such a great desire and will to attain, why does one not do what is required? For you should be certain of   50 and hold firmly to the belief that you have no other course of action to take except to remember that if you love God, God will love you. Serve Him well: He will reward you for it. Fear Him: He will make you feel secure. Honor Him: He will honor you. Ask of Him and you will receive much from Him. Pray to Him for mercy: He will pardon you. Call on Him when   55 you are in danger: He will save you from it. Turn to Him when you are afraid, and He will protect you. Pray to Him for comfort, and He will comfort you. Believe totally in Him and He will bring you to salvation in His glorious company and His sweet paradise which will last for ever without end. He who is willing to act thus will save his body and his soul, and 60 he who does the opposite will be damned in soul and body. Pray to God for him who is the author of this book.

Explicit Charni, Charny.

Notes to the Translation

Abbreviations used in the notes

LK: Lancelot do Lac: The Non-Cyclic Old French Prose Romance, ed. Elspeth Kennedy. 2 vols. Oxford, 1980.

LM: Lancelot: roman en prose du XIIIe siècle, ed. Alexandre Micha. 9 vols. Paris-Geneva, 1978–83.

LOC: Livre de l'ordre de chevallerie, the medieval French translation of Ramon Llull, *Le Libre del orde de cavalleria*, in *Obres de Ramon Lull*, ed. Antoni M. Alcover, Mateu Obrador, Bennassar. Palma de Mallorca: Comissio Editora Lulliana, 1906, vol. I, 249–291.

OC: L'Ordene de chevalerie, in *Le Roman des eles, by Raoul de Hodenc and L'Ordene de chevalerie*, ed. Keith Busby. Utrecht Publications in General and Comparative Literature 17, Amsterdam, 1983.

Perceforest 1: *Le Roman de Perceforest, première partie*, ed. Jane Taylor. Geneva, 1979.

Perceforest 3: *Perceforest, troisième partie*, ed. Gilles Roussineau. 2 vols. Geneva, 1988.

Perceforest 4: *Perceforest, quatrième partie*, ed. Gilles Roussineau. 2 vols. Geneva, 1987.

Except where otherwise stated, all the translations of quotations from other works are by Elspeth Kennedy.

5.9–12

honneur/honor, coupled as it is here with *heritage*/inheritance, may well still have the meaning of land held as a fief.

7.8–10

glaive can mean "lance" (as it does in *fer de glaive*, 7.8) or sword; in the fourteenth century it can also mean "infantry weapon," presumably inappropriate here.

12.4

The practice of *fin' amour* (a medieval expression) or "courtly love," a term invented in the nineteenth century describes the idealized form of love service celebrated in lyric and romance. The true love of a knight for a noble lady as a source of inspiration for great deeds is a theme explored in the Arthurian romances, especially the Prose *Lancelot*. See, for example, the message sent by the Lady of the

Lake to the young Lancelot that he must devote himself to a love which will increase his honor, not diminish it (*LK*, 205–6).

12.15–18

For the honor a lady can win through her love for a great knight, see the Lady of the Lake's words to Guinevere: And you can boast of that which no lady could ever boast of before, for you are the companion of the most worthy man in the world and the lady of the best knight in the world (*Lancelot of the Lake*, trans. Corin Corley, Oxford, 1989). For the lady's duty toward the good knight who loves her, see also 20.37–42.

17.3

coureurs: light horsemen used as scouts or foragers.

17.16

The meaning of the term in this context is obscure.

17.18–19

truyes, "sows," and *chas*, "cats," are roofed mobile structures often used to cover mining operations. The *baffroi*, "belfry," a siege tower, could also be used for this. We can find no reference to *buyre* as an item of siege equipment; the term usually means "vase;" it seems likely that within this context it is used to denote a mobile protective structure, possibly vase-shaped, which served the same purpose as cats and sows, as these devices were called by many names. See Jim Bradbury, *The Medieval Siege* (Woodbridge, 1992), 271.

17.44

The phrase *es honorables* is unusual; the translation given represents the probable meaning of the sentence.

19.195–97

To be compared with *LK*, 30.32–31.9, where Claudas explains why he has given up love: he wants to live for a long time and therefore does not want to love (*amer par amors*), for this would make him want to surpass the whole world and thus put his life in danger; but he admits: "il ne puet estre tres preuz d'armes se il n'aimme tres leialment" (no one can achieve worth in the pursuit of arms if he does not love loyally).

19.197–216

The need for secrecy in love receives great emphasis in the medieval lyric and romance. For example, in a short thirteenth-century romance, *La chastelaine de Vergi,* a knight is granted the love of the *chastelaine* on condition that the love remains secret; he is forced to reveal the love to his lord, and as a result both he and his lady die. The reference by Geoffroi de Charny to Guinevere in this passage would link up with the Prose *Lancelot*, where the hero always remains silent about his love for the Queen. For example, when imprisoned by the Lady of Malehaut, he refuses to name the one he loves *par amors*, although by doing so he would have obtained his freedom (*LK*, 303).

20.37–42
For the honor to be gained and the duty owed by the lady to the good knight who loves her, see also 12.15–20 and note.

24.75–81
For the sources for this account of the origin of emperors, kings, and princes, see note to 25.1–6.

25.1–6
The explanation of the origin of emperors, kings and princes appears to have been drawn from Ramon Llull's account of the origin of knights. According to Llull, after the Fall of Man those with the greatest physical and moral qualities were chosen and set apart from other men as defenders of justice and of the Holy Church. Charny would also have found a similar account in another text he knew well, the Prose *Lancelot*, itself the main source for Llull's version of the origin of knights. See *LOC*, p. 254, where the people are divided into thousands and from each thousand one man is elected, he who is "plus loyal, plus fort et de plus noble courage et mieulz enseigné que tous les autres" (the most loyal, the strongest and the noblest in heart and the best educated of all men). See also *LK*, 142, where, as in Charny, there is no division into thousands, but the men are chosen for the same types of qualities: "Ce furent li grant et li fort et li bel et li legier et li leial et li hardi, cil qui des bontez del cuer et del cors estoient plain" (These were the big and the strong and the handsome and the nimble and the loyal and the courageous, those who were full of the qualities of the heart and of the body).

25.6–16
The heavy responsibility resting on the shoulders of the men chosen to be emperors, kings and princes recalls the following passage from the Lady of the Lake's explanation of chivalry in the Prose *Lancelot*, *LK*, 142: "Mais la chevalerie ne lor fu pas donee an bades ne por neiant, ençois lor en fu mis desor les cox mout granz faissiaus" (but knighthood was not given to them frivolously and for no good reason; on the contrary, a heavy burden was put on their shoulders). The obligations of those chosen for high office, the charges put upon them and the moral qualities and behavior expected of them in Charny and traditionally required of kings are similar to those demanded of the men chosen to be knights in *LK*. Indeed, in medieval literature in general, the advice given to kings on their duties and that given to knights on theirs frequently overlap.

25.17–18
"Si estoient esleuz et faiz pour amer, doubter et servir Dieu et toutes ses oevres." To be compared with Llull, *LOC*, 268, IV, 2: "Car sans amer et doubter Dieu nul

homme n'est digne d'entrer en l'ordre de chevallerie (For no man who does not love and fear God is worthy to enter the order of knighthood.) Llull and the Prose *Lancelot* both emphasize the duty of the knight to protect the Holy Church, which cannot use arms to defend itself, *LOC,* 257–58, III, §2; *LK,* 143–45.

25.25–27

For the duty of rulers to see that justice is upheld, cf. Llull (*LOC,* 259, III, 8), and *LK,* 142. However, both these texts also emphasize the duty of the knight to help the King in the maintenance of justice. In *LK,* the adventures which the Knights of the Round Table undertake often concern the maintenance of justice in the lands over which Arthur is lord (see Kennedy, *Lancelot and the Grail,* 79–80, 102–7). Arthur is told that it is his duty to see that justice is done (*LK,* 283), but that he needs the help of *li bas gentil homme* to maintain his land (*LK,* 285).

25.29–30

For the need to be prepared to journey constantly, cf. *LK,* 286–87, where Arthur is told by a holy man that he must travel round all his *boenes viles* so that the great and the humble can seek justice at his court. Knights errant also are constantly promising not to spend more than one night in a place until they have completed the object of their quest. See, for example, Gauvain's oath (*LK,* 220) and the Lady of the Lake's instructions to the young Lancelot before he leaves for Arthur's court (*LK,* 154). See also Perceval's oath in *Le Roman de Perceval ou le Conte du Graal,* ed. William Roach (Geneva, 1956), ll. 4728–40.

25.34–37

To be *large* (generous) is a traditional quality demanded of both knight and king.

35.75–79

Note that the blind Samson's action in pulling down the pillars is here condemned as a misuse of strength, although in the biblical account there is no such condemnation: Samson prays to God to give him strength to pull down the pillars so that he might avenge himself on the Philistines. See Judges xvii: 25–30.

35.79–83

For Absalom hanging by his hair from a tree, see 2 Samuel xviii: 9

35.83–87

For Solomon's worship of idols, see 1 Kings, ii.

35.87–92

For Peter's threefold denial of Christ, see Matthew, xxvii; Mark, xiv; Luke, xxii.

35.96–123

Caesar's assassination: Dr. Jane Taylor has drawn our attention to a similar account of Caesar's death to be found in the fourteenth-century romance *Perceforest.* According to the *Perceforest*, the leader behind the plot had special *greffes* made from metal (*greffes* are styles, pointed instruments used for writing on wax tablets). Caesar was given a warning letter on his way to the Senate; he took it in his hand, but did not read it. Before the conspirators entered the Senate House, they were given these styles under the pretense that they could use them to record Caesar's pronouncement.

35.152

Judas Maccabeus is cited as one who benefited from divine assistance in a prayer for the recipient of the knightly sword in the late thirteenth-century pontifical of Guillaume Durand. See Jean Flori, "Chevalerie et liturgie: remise des armes et vocabulaire "chevaleresque" dans les sources liturgiques du IXe au XIVe siècle," *Le Moyen Age* 84 (1978), pp. 247–78 and 409–42 (438). There are many allusions to him in medieval literature as one of the first of the great knights; they culminate in his promotion to the rank of one of the Nine Worthies in the *Voeux du Paon* of Jacques de Longuyon (1312). See D. A. Trotter, "Judas Maccabeus, Charlemagne and the oriflamme," *Medium Aevum* 54 (1985): 127–31.

36.4–57

This account of the knighting ceremony follows very closely that to be found in *OC*, 108–12.

40.35–36

I have based my emendation on the pattern of the following sentence in the Brussels MS: *Et qui fait les faiz d'armes plus pour avoir la grace de Dieu et pour les ames sauver que pour la gloire de ce monde.*

41.14–15

bien escorche qui le pié tient, translated as "he does mischief enough who helps mischief." The literal translation would be "he who holds the foot also takes part in the flaying." Cotgrave's rendering of the proverb has been used.

42.170–71

It is not quite clear whether it is the *riches aournemens* or the *chetiz corps* which are the subject of the clause *qui n'ont heure ne terme de durer*.

Suggestions for Further Reading

SOURCES

Bernard of Clairvaux. *Treatises III: On Grace and Free Choice: Praise of the New Knighthood.* Trans. Daniel O'Donovan and Conrad Greenia. In *The Works of Bernard of Clairvaux*, vol. 7. Christian Fathers Series 19. Kalamazoo, Mich., 1977.

Chandos Herald. *Life of the Black Prince, by the Herald of Sir John Chandos.* Ed. Mildred K. Pope and Eleanor C. Lodge. Oxford, 1910, reprint New York, 1974.

L'Histoire de Guillaume le Marechal. Ed. Paul Meyer. 3 vols. Paris, 1891–1901.

History of William Marshall. Ed. A. J. Holden, Stewart Gregory, and David Crouch. Vol. 1, *Text and Translation (ll. 1 -10031).* Anglo-Norman Text Society Occasional Papers 4. London, 2002.

Jean de Venette. *The Chronicle of Jean de Venette.* Trans. Jean Birdsall, ed. Richard Newhall. New York, 1953.

Lancelot do Lac: The Non-Cyclic Old French Prose Romance. Ed. Elspeth Kennedy. 2 vols. Oxford, 1980.

Lancelot-Grail: The Old French Arthurian Vulgate and Post-Vulgate in Translation. Ed. Norris J. Lacy. New York, 1993–96.

Lancelot of the Lake. Trans. Corin Corley. Oxford, 1989.

Llull, Ramon. *The Book of the Ordre of Chyvalry.* Trans. William Caxton, ed. Alfred T. P. Byles. Early English Text Society 168. London, 1926.

Malory, Sir Thomas. *Works.* 3 vols. 3rd ed. Ed. Eugene Vinaver, rev. P. J. C. Field. Oxford, 1990.

Perlesvaus. The High Book of the Grail: A Translation of the Thirteenth-Century Romance of Perlesvaus. Trans. Nigel Bryant. Cambridge, 1978.

The Quest of the Holy Grail. Trans. Pauline M. Matarasso. Harmondsworth, 1969.

Raoul de Houdenc. *Le Roman des eles, by Raoul de Houdenc and The Anonymous Ordenede la chevalerie.* Ed. Keith Busby. Utrecht Publications in General and Comparative Literature 17. Amsterdam, 1983.

SECONDARY WORKS

Barber, Richard and Juliet Barker. *Tournaments, Jousts, Chivalry, and Pageants in the Middle Ages.* New York, 1989.

Boulton, D'Arcy Dacre Jonathan. *The Knights of the Crown: The Monarchical Orders of Knighthood in Later Medieval Europe, 1325–1520.* New York, 1987.

Contamine, Philippe. "Geoffroy de Charny (début de XIVe siècle-1356), 'Le plus prudhomme etle plus vaillant de tous les autres.'" In *Histoire et société: Mélanges offerts à Georges Duby*, vol. 2, *Le tenancier, le fidèle et le citoyen*. Aix-en-Provence, 1992. 107–21.

Crouch, David. *William Marshal: Court, Career and Chivalry in the Angevin Empire, 1147–1219*. London, 1990.

Dale, W. S. A. "The Shroud of Turin: Relic or Icon?" *Nuclear Instruments and Methods in Physics Research* B29 (1987), 187–92.

Duby, Georges. *William Marshal: The Flower of Chivalry*. Trans. Richard Howard. New York, 1985.

Erdmann, Carl. *The Origin of the Idea of Crusade*. Trans. Marshal W. Baldwin and Walter Goffart. Princeton, N.J., 1977.

Hewitt, Herbert James. *The Black Prince's Expedition of 1355–1357*. Manchester, 1958.

———. *The Organization of War Under Edward III, 1338–1362*. Manchester, 1966.

Kaeuper, Richard W. *Chivalry and Violence in Medieval Europe*. Oxford, 1999.

———. "The Social Meaning of Chivalry in Romance." In *The Cambridge Companion to Medieval Romance*, ed. Robert L. Krueger. Cambridge, 2000.

———. War, *Justice and Public Order: England and France in the Later Middle Ages*. Oxford, 1988.

Kaeuper, Richard W., and Elspeth Kennedy. *The Book of Chivalry of Geoffroi de Charny: Text, Context, and Translation*. Philadelphia, 1996.

Keen, Maurice. *Chivalry*. New Haven, Conn., 1984.

———. "Chivalry, Nobility, and the Man-at-Arms." In *War, Literature and Politics in the Late Middle Ages*, ed. C. T. Allmand. Liverpool, 1976.

Kennedy, Elspeth M. "Geoffroi de Charny's *Livre de chevalerie* and the Knights of the Round Table." In *Medieval Knighthood V: Papers from the Sixth Strawberry Hill Conference*, ed. Stephen Church and Ruth Harvey. Woodbridge, 1995. 221–42.

———. "The Knight as Reader of Arthurian Romance." In *Culture and the King: The Social Implications of the Arthurian Legend, Essays in Honor of Valerie M. Lagorio*, ed. Martin B. Schichtman and James P. Carley. New York, 1995. 70–90.

———. *Lancelot and the Grail: A Study of the Prose Lancelot*. Oxford, 1980.

———. "The Quest for Identity and the Importance of Lineage in Thirteenth-Century ProseRomance." In *The Ideals and Practice of Medieval Knighthood II: Papers from the Third Strawberry Hill Conference*, ed. Christopher Harper-Bill and Ruth Harvey. Woodbridge, 1988.

———. "Theory and Practice: The Portrayal of Chivalry in the Prose Lancelot, Geoffrey de Charny, and Froissart." In *Froissart Across the Genres*, ed. Donald Maddox and Sara Sturm-Maddox. Gainesville, Fl., 1998. 179–94.

Strickland, Matthew. *War and Chivalry: The Conduct and Perception of War in England and Normandy, 1066–1217*. Cambridge, 1996.

Sumption, Jonathan. *The Hundred Years War*. 2 vols. Vol. 1, *Trial by Battle*. Philadelphia, 1999.

Vale, Malcolm. *War and Chivalry: Warfare and Aristocratic Culture in England, France, and Burgundy at the End of the Middle Ages*. Norwich, 1981.

Acknowledgments

JEROME SINGERMAN of the University of Pennsylvania Press suggested this new book as a means of bringing Geoffroi de Charny to a wider audience. Bruce Franklin and Alison Anderson skillfully saw it through the press. My warm thanks go to all three.

Thanks also to several people at the University of Rochester. I appreciated the work of Peter Shirtzinger and Benjamin Tejblum as undergraduate research assistants. Their help was made possible through an imaginative program instituted by Theodore Brown and Joan Rubin in the Department of History. Alan Unsworth, History Bibliographer in Rush Rhees Library found even the most obscure sources, as always. Michael Egolf, my research assistant, meticulously proofread the historical introduction.

I am happy to repeat my gratitude to Elspeth Kennedy for her wonderful rendering of Geoffroi de Charny's difficult Middle French into readable English without losing the presence of the knightly author.

R.W. Kaeuper